D0449146

What people are saying about Linda, Jim, Tony and their fine work

"Linda McKissack is one of the most learning-based, business-smart real estate agents I know. In just eight years she went from being a struggling new agent to a 7th Level Millionaire with a real estate business doing over 300 transactions a year. She has truly turned her real estate practice into a business; and she is teaching other agents to do the same. What Linda shares is powerful, practical and very credible—she's done it!"

—**DAVE JENKS**, Co-author of *The Millionaire Real Estate Agent*,
Vice President of Keller Williams Realty International,
Master trainer of real estate top producers for over 25 years

"These principles will positively effect my business simply by realizing that everything I do is a presentation."

—**JIM CORTWELL**, Southland Title

"Linda McKissack was one of the first Mega Agents to join our company. Keller Williams Realty would not be where it is today without her influence, her passion, and her pioneering spirit. Linda embodies the qualities of the ultimate, top performer. She is committed to doing her best at all times. Linda learns the most that she can to become a master of the subjects that she needs to master, and is willing to share the gifts of her learning with others."

—**MARK WILLIS**, CEO, Keller Williams Realty

"You need to hear and be a part of what Tony offers. It will change your life for the better."

—**NILS MINER, JR.** Centry

"Linda McKissack is a *master presenter* and master real estate agent! Excellence is her forté. . .one can learn from the *Master*!"
—**MO ANDERSON**, Vice Chairman of the Board Keller Williams Realty

"Linda is a true professional and she knows the business!! I first heard her on the Star Power tapes and she has definitely lived up to her reputation."

"Wonderful!! First time I attended a course that I have learned so much and I have definitely attended plenty. I've been in the business over 30 years."

"Thanks for giving me a glimpse of business strategies that I have never seen before."

"Linda is an excellent "teacher". Keeps class moving, answers questions quickly and concisely. Best class I've ever taken. Handouts excellent!"

"Great energy! Great Ideas!"

"Whether you are in sales or are the CEO of a billion-dollar corporation, let Tony Jeary be your personal coach."
—**MARK VICTOR HANSEN**, author of *Chicken Soup For The Soul*

"Tony Jeary is the right teacher."

—ZIG ZIGLAR, author of *See You At The Top*

"I encourage you to try the Jeary Theory—practical,
effective steps to make your presentations effective."

—JOHN C. MAXWELL, author of *The 21 Irrefutable Laws of Leadership*

"Occasionally, a book comes along that inspires you to
greatness AND gives you the practical know how to
accomplish your goals. *Presentation Mastery* has it all.
If you want to guarantee your success in the real estate
business. . .or in any business, read this book!"

—V. JOHN ALEXANDROV, Author of the Best Selling *Affirmations
of Wealth, Your Spiritual Gold Mind,* and *The Money Chi.*

"Tony shows us presenting is not about being on stage,
it is about coummunicating our ideas in ways that
inspire the enthusiastic support of others. . ."

—DENIS WAITLEY, author of *The Psychology of Winning*

"It is a pleasure to acknowledge
Tony Jeary and his fantastic work. . ."

—DR. ROBERT SCHULLER

Presentation Mastery™

for

REALTORS®

FOREWORD BY **GARY KELLER**

Presentation Mastery™

for

Build Your Own Brand
Present Your Best Self
Increase Your Income

REALTORS®

LINDA
AND **JIM**
McKISSACK
& TONY JEARY
MR. PRESENTATION™

McKissack Group Publishing
Flower Mound, Texas

Presentation Mastery for Realtors

Published by
McKissack Group Publishing
3605 Yucca Drive, Ste. 202, Flower Mound, TX 75028
(972) 874-7400

www.PresentationMasteryforRealtors.com

Copyright © Linda and Jim McKissack and Tony Jeary

All rights reserved. No part of this book may be reproduced by any mechanical, photographic, or electronic process, or in the form of a phonographic recording, nor may it be stored in a retrieval system, transmitted, or otherwise be copied for public or private use without prior written permission by the publisher.

Mr. Presentation™ and Branding Matrix are trademarks of Tony Jeary High Performance Resources, LLC (TJHPR). Presentation Mastery™ is a trademark of Tony Jeary High Performance Resources LLC and George Lowe and Greg Kaiser. All TJHPR trademarks appearing in *Presentation Mastery for Realtors* are the property of TJHPR and all rights in those trademarks are reserved. All other trademarks appearing in *Presentation Mastery for Realtors* are the property of their respective owners.

ISBN-13: 978-0-9799059-0-2
ISBN-10: 0-9799059-0-7

Cover and Interior Design: Desktop Miracles, Inc.

Printed in the United States of America

Publisher's Cataloging-In-Publication Data
(Prepared by The Donohue Group, Inc.)

McKissack, Linda.
　　Presentation mastery for realtors : build your own brand, present your best self, increase your income / Linda and Jim McKissack & Tony Jeary ; foreword by Gary Keller.
　　　　p. ; cm.
　　ISBN-13: 978-0-9799059-0-2
　　ISBN-10: 0-9799059-0-7

　　1. Real estate business. 2. Real estate agents. 3. Business presentations. 4. Success in business. I. McKissack, Jim. II. Jeary, Tony, 1961– III. Keller, Gary. IV. Title.
HD1375 .M35 2007

333.33/023

Table of Contents

> Do you want to reach your goals more effectively and grow to new heights no matter what level of success you've achieved? You are presenting virtually every time you interact with someone, and your presentations—both to yourself and to the world around you—play a huge role in your success.

SECTION ONE

Building Your Real Estate Business Through Presentation Mastery

Life is a series of presentations. Successful people—whether they are real estate agents, corporate executives, stay-at-home moms, or fulfilling any other roles in life—have mastered at some point along the way the art of presentation. Chapters One through Four teach core presentation mastery skills that will help you catapult your business toward the success you've always wanted.

Presenting yourself well from a branding perspective gives your business top billing with prospective clients and takes you to the highest level as a real estate agent. If you want to build a successful business—whether that is a valuable asset to be sold, a legacy to be handed down to your family, or some other measure—you must build it to your brand. Learn the secrets of positioning your brand to put your business "top of mind" in your market, and see how presenting a consistent message about your company draws clients to your door.

Our years of experience and success have taught us what works
and what doesn't in marketing your real estate business. Audit
your marketing collateral against our list of tools to see if you
are presenting your brand for the highest impact. Learn how
to leverage your brand with the right tools for you and how to
make all of these pieces fit together to present the same "family"
appearance, appeal, and message, so people will remember
you when the time is right.

It's almost impossible in today's world to present your business
successfully without a presence on the web. Building your website to clearly reflect your consistent brand will make it one of
the most powerful tools in your marketing arsenal. See how
we generate hundreds of leads each year from our website and
provide a powerful resource for our clients as well. Let us show
you how to join the elite group of top real estate agents who
market on the web. And you might need to prepare yourself for
a paradigm shift: You can actually develop this vital tool in 48
hours for less than $250!

Everywhere you go, you have one-on-one encounters, whether
it is at the grocery store, at your child's school, or at a restaurant. And, of course, networking plays a major role in a real
estate agents success. So what do you say on these impromptu
encounters? How can you plant seeds that will later produce a
harvest? Learn how to maximize every opportunity by connecting with potential clients on the spot.

SECTION TWO

Servicing Your Clients
Through Presentation Mastery

No matter how well you brand and market your business, as a real estate professional you must move toward becoming a master presenter in four key areas for your business to succeed: 1) securing the listing, 2) negotiating the offer, 3) presenting at the closing table, and 4) presenting after the sale. Chapters Five through Seven will teach you the presentation essentials to provide the highest level of service to your clients.

Part of the philosophy of presentation mastery is holding effective meetings with prospective clients. The successful agent no longer operates with a "show-and-tell" mentality, but makes the sale based on an assessment of the clients' needs and meeting their expectations. Let us show you how we have mastered the consultative approach that results in a win/win outcome, whether we are securing the listing from a seller or negotiating an offer for a buyer.

When clients come to the closing table, the last thing they want is a surprise. As their real estate agent you want them to feel good about the purchase of their new home or the accomplishment of the sale, and nothing will kill their enthusiasm more than a last-minute hitch. The key to presenting well at the closing table is diligent preparation. We'll give you tools that will make your clients love you and want to send people your way!

A real estate agents dream clients are those that stay with them for a lifetime of real estate needs and refer them to all of their friends and family. By presenting effectively to the client after the sale, you can establish this kind of relationship. We'll provide simple practices that will teach you how to retain your clients by communicating with them through a three-prong follow-up system: by mail, by phone, and electronically.

We have reached a level of achievement in our lives for which we are very grateful. Yes, we have worked hard and mastered the art of presentation, and it has brought us to this level. But we can't discount the fact that other people have given into our lives, as well, and helped us to find the reason for building our business. We have discovered that there is never a negative repercussion from giving to other people. The Real Estate Industry today, as a whole, has become greedy, and we want to do what we can to help change that. We hope your life is enriched by reading this book, and that you achieve greater success through all the presentations you make in life, both personally and professionally.

Foreword

BY GARY KELLER

When I first met Jim and Linda McKissack I could tell right away they were incredibly special and wonderfully talented. These two had established a remarkably successful real estate business in Denton, Texas, a place not known for its real estate market, and yet there they were.

That was more than ten years ago. In the years since I've had the pleasure of getting to know them and observe them in their work both up close and from a distance. The more I got to know Jim and Linda the less it surprised me that they were able to reach such a phenomenal level of success despite facing many tough challenges in their market. Their genuine honesty, generous spirit, hunger for knowledge, and eagerness to share what they know with others is something that continues to impress me.

For anyone that is interested in learning about what it takes to achieve success in the real estate sales business, Jim and Linda provide an excellent example to follow. Jim and Linda are true students of the art of business, sales, and customer service. They know how to develop a winning game plan and how to stick with it. They recognize the importance of delivering powerful presentations and making the accompanying scripts the foundation of the language they use with their clients and team. To Jim and Linda, what you say and what you do are the same thing and the essence of who you are as a businessperson and real estate agent.

Jim and Linda have something worthwhile to share, they have earned the right to share it, and have developed the skills to share it well. Enjoy.

Acknowledgements

How in the world do you ever acknowledge everyone who has contributed to this book when the best and worst parts of your life have been filled with teachers—some teaching what to do and some teaching what not to do?

Everything we have accomplished has been because of our Creator and the people in our lives. Let's just say we are enormously grateful for all who have contributed to our success. We appreciate our kids for the sacrifices they made for us to be able to contribute the time needed to succeed in real estate and business. We appreciate each other for our commitment in our marriage and our life together as best friends, spouses, parents and business partners and for the balance we add to each other's lives.

To the mentors and influencers we have been blessed with from the beginning until now and the ones yet to come into our lives, you have our unending thanks:

- Mike Ferry for being willing to tell us the hard stuff.
- Howard Brinton for helping us to see the stars and become stars.
- Tony Jeary for his inspiration and giving spirit in co-authoring this book and sharing with us the secrets of a successful speaking business.

- Dr. Fred Grosse for helping us to understand that as real estate agents we had some major issues; that we had jobs not businesses; that we need multiple streams of income and that every 7 years we should change up what we are doing or do something different to recharge that passion we have for the business; and for teaching us how to be tall poppies in a herd world.
- Our Fred Family from our Mastermind group—for five years you each contributed to our lives and this book, and for this we are grateful: Gary and Nikki Ubaldini, Joe and Mary Harker, Roger and Tony Tygart, Art and Anna Kleimer, John and Patty Ancona, Tony Dicello and Diana Kokoszka, Ray McCarthy and Terry Moerler, Ron and Melinda Garber, Phil and Marsha Kelly, Jim and Mary Jean Nussbaum, and Dr. Fred and Victoria Grosse.
- Gary Keller for being the greatest example of a leader anyone could have; for always living God, Family, and Business so we could see it could be done and still succeed at a high level; for reinventing the real estate business for the agent and providing bigger opportunities than we could have created for ourselves; for always doing what you say you'll do; for always being our mentor and our friend. God Bless you for all you have done for real estate agents and their futures and for allowing us to leave a legacy. Thanks also to our incredible Keller Williams Realty family.
- Don Arnold, for his expertise, wisdom and insight of working with builders and new construction.
- And last, but by no means least of all, thanks to Brad and Susan McKissack and the entire McKissack Group, for helping us to be successful in serving the wonderful people of Denton and the surrounding areas in their pursuit of home ownership. You mean everything to us.

Our heartfelt thanks to all.

LINDA AND JIM MCKISSACK

Introduction

Do you believe you can be more successful in your life and business than you already are? If you do, you've come to the right place! One thing we have learned over the years is that there are four major obstacles that can derail your success. If you're not where you want to be, we suspect it is because of one or more of these reasons:

1. You don't believe it is possible
   (or perhaps cannot envision the goal)
2. You don't know what to do or how to do it
3. You have not yet made it a habit
   (are not disciplined enough)
4. You have not put it into a system

My husband Jim and I have worked hard to build a world-class real estate company, but it didn't come fast and there weren't any shortcuts. We made a decision to change our thinking and our lifestyle, and rose out of $600,000 in debt to build a Real Estate business with over $60 million in sales annually. A large part of our success has been our ability to understand how to make effective presentations that could overcome obstacles, help build our business, and provoke buyers and sellers to want to do business with us. Making presentations truly is a skill, and it can be learned.

As we share with you our secrets, we will be teaching you how to overcome the four obstacles above by mastering your presentations to yourself, your market, your team, your family, and others in your world. There's just no getting around it: our lives really are a series of presentations, and our success is a direct result of our mastering the presentations we make on a daily basis. We believe, however, that there is yet a deeper concept involved in mastering our presentations, and that the most important presentations we will ever make are those that involve the heart.

Let me explain. As I look back over our combined 35 years in the real estate industry, one concept keeps coming to mind—the resounding truth that building a successful career in real estate is really all about the relationships you develop. Those relationships—with your clients, your broker, your employees, your peers, and, most importantly, your family—are forged and nurtured by the deep presentations of your heart. If your presentations to those people do not come from your heart; the relationships will be shallow, meaningless, and temporary.

Our mentor and coach Gary Keller says, "No one succeeds alone." You *need* relationships with others if you are to be successful! It's very important that you choose well those with whom you spend your time and involve in your business. It's equally important that you nurture them into strong, long-lasting relationships. To build successful relationships, you must get "on purpose" about how you present yourself. Successful relationships are built on trust, honesty, integrity, and just doing the right things. They are built on your values and beliefs, on how you treat people and what you say, and on your resolve to do what you say you are going to do.

Amazingly, as you build those strong, trusting relationships, you will soon notice that new opportunities will begin to appear in your life. Learn to recognize and seize these opportunities for what they really are—blessings! Sometimes what appears to be something that is happening *to* you is actually a "blessing" that happens *for* you!

Our co-author and friend Tony Jeary is coach to the world's top CEOs and the author of several books. He's also a world-renowned motivational speaker who has been on the cover of several magazines, and presented in various countries—so his presentation skills are second to none. Tony is an expert at guiding others how to become Presentation Masters! As real estate professionals, we're presenting each and every day—bumping into clients in the grocery store, post office, and of course, at listing presentations! Every human interaction is an opportunity for a presentation to a prospective client, and there's no one better than Tony to teach us how to become so effective, that no one can say no. Tony's principles on presentation skills can transform your business, and make you a people magnet that attracts buyers and sellers time and again.

In his book *Success Acceleration* Tony writes about a principle called The Belief Window, and we delve into that deeper in this book. The theory of the Belief Window is that whether we know it or not, we all conduct our lives and make decisions based on our principles. *If* those principles are accurate, they will help us make right choices, so understanding how our principles govern our decisions is one of the most dynamic concepts we can use to quicken our success.

Tony coaches people to understand how powerful Belief Windows are, and how understanding and embracing them can accelerate their business success. He writes; "Your outlook on the world around you is determined by your *belief windows*. Your clients, colleagues, family and friends all filter life and process information through the principles they began forming from birth. These principles create a belief window that affects everything someone sees, hears, and experiences. Each one of us forms our life "rules" based on those individual beliefs, and then we establish a behavior pattern according to our rules. Unless we are operating our lives with flawless principles, we are probably not achieving the level of success we want."

The Belief Window is just one of the ideas we present in this book, as a component of building and enhancing your effectiveness and communication skills. Understanding this foundational concept can catapult you toward quickening achievement, and place you far ahead of your competitors.

Believing that you can be successful as a real estate professional is one thing; believing that you are in the right business is another. If you think you are doing something "to" someone, instead of "for" someone, you will never succeed in this business. It's a matter of changing what's in your belief window. We will show you how to service your clients with a consultative approach based upon your customers' needs, and you can come away from every sale satisfied that you have done a great service for your client.

If your challenge is knowing what to do or how to do it, or developing habits or systems, this book is for you. We've worked hard and learned much for over 18 years in the real estate business and have reached a high level of success that we hope you can benefit from—principles that you can apply to your own business, to achieve a breakthrough this year!

ONE

Building Your
Real Estate Business
Through
Presentation Mastery

Presenting
Your Brand

Caught off guard, it took us a minute to realize what had just happened. Jim and I had been walking through our local mall when suddenly a clerk in one of the stores walked up to us and threw both thumbs into the air as if to give us the thumbs up! Somewhat confused, we haltingly gave him the thumbs-up sign in return and walked on. Then it dawned on us—for the first time someone had recognized us from our branding efforts for what we *do*, and not for who we *were*. We had been running a cable advertisement in which we stood behind one of our signs and gave the big thumbs up to represent the sign of accomplishment for getting another home sold. Amazingly, the thumbs-up sign quickly became contagious throughout our market, even to the point that our daughter asked us to please not run that commercial again. At ten years old, she was not really into the name recognition she was receiving even at school. But obviously our market was because this kind of recognition was something that would continue to happen to us from that day forward.

To this day, people in our area know us because they *recognize our brand. We have learned to present ourselves well from a branding perspective, and this method of presentation has been one of the highest contributing factors to our success.* Everything we do as real estate agents is done in the form of a presentation, whether we are prospecting, marketing, negotiating, or selling. And how well we *present* determines our success. But how well we *present our brand* determines, to a large degree, the ease with which that success is achieved.

We have learned to position our brand to make our business "top of mind" in our market, and it draws clients to our door. If you ask people within our market area who they think of when they think "real estate," many will tell you that they think of us first. An agent in one of our franchise offices in Indianapolis, Indiana, was selling a home to someone who was moving there from Denton, Texas, where we live. The agent asked her client if she had ever heard of the McKissacks, and her response was, "*Everyone* has heard of the McKissacks!" The client went on to say, "If I wanted to sell my home fast, that's who I would call." When people call in to our office, we ask them, "How did you choose the McKissack Group?" The number one reply we receive is, "They're *everywhere!*" When you get that kind of feedback, you know your business has reached "top of mind" in your market.

Presenting yourself well from a branding perspective lays the foundation to take you to the highest level as a real estate agent. In the process of building our business, we discovered some very important secrets that helped us position our brand to bring about the height of success we enjoy today. As we share these secrets with you, you will see how everything you do affects the way you present your brand, from the priority you place on learning to the way you present yourself and your business to your market and the way you service your clients.

The 12 Secrets for Presenting Your Brand

Jim and I have learned that there are 12 crucial secrets for presenting your brand. They are:

#1: Learn from and model others

#2: Present yourself as successful—both in actions and appearance

#3: Choose a name with room to grow

#4: Communicate your brand in everything you do, and be consistent

#5: Be bold and different

#6: Tactfully drip, or touch people often so they remember you

#7: Choose a motto or a theme to use in your marketing

#8: Leverage your photo

#9: Reinforce your brand with good service and added value

#10: Present that you are successful at the specific things your clients want to accomplish

#11: Consistently present using third-party testimonials

#12: Present your brand to appeal to the different behavioral styles

1. **Learn from and Model Others.** Making the decision to be a learning-based business early on in our real estate career has turned out to be our best secret weapon. What does this have to do with presenting your brand? Branding is a form of presentation, and as a rule, when you start in the real estate business, you are thrust out on your own with very little training. That's exactly what happened to us, so we decided to seek outside real estate trainers to help us learn the concepts and get ideas about how to build our business. *One of the most important things we learned was how to present our brand, and that has been an investment that has paid off—handsomely.* Over the years, we have constantly sought knowledge about the real estate business from people who have already been out there and made their mistakes and then learned to do it right. It just made sense to us because it shortened our learning curve and saved us a massive amount of time and money that we would have wasted had we chosen to do it strictly by trial and error. If you want to go to the highest level, training is an investment you simply can't afford to sacrifice. Present yourself—in your own mind and to the world—as the CEO of your own company, rather than an employee. *You* must first be convinced that your work is a business, rather than a job—and that you are the CEO of that business. Business owners take responsibility for marketing and building their own companies, rather than expecting other people to do it for them. If you opened a clothing boutique or a computer equipment and supply company, there would be certain things you would have to do, as the owner, to let people know you are in business. It's no different in the real estate business. It's YOUR business. You can't expect your broker to build it for you.

There are only two ways to get clients for your real estate business: prospecting (seeking clients) and marketing (attracting clients). The best real estate businesses are a healthy combination of both: marketing-based, prospecting and referral-enhanced. The first reality check comes when you realize that *you*, as the owner and CEO of your own company, have to perform both of those functions.

There are actually well over 168 tasks that Real Estate Agents have to perform in relation to each sale. (You can access the entire list at www.PresentationMasteryForRealtors.com.) As you begin to understand that you are the CEO of your own company, and that "if it is to be, it's up to me," it's easy to become overwhelmed and confused with the enormity of the job. It might help to know that, in reality, all 168 tasks can be separated into four basic functions: marketing and prospecting, as we have already mentioned, plus negotiating and selling.

As CEO, you will also need to keep close tabs on all the numbers it takes to be successful: the number of leads that actually turn into appointments, the number of contacts you have to make before you get an appointment, the number of appointments that turn into actual listings, and the number of listings that turn into actual dollars for your company. Another number to watch is the percentage of your repeat business. If that percentage gets too high, it means you are not making your branding work for you. If most of your business is repeat and referral, you are obviously not generating a lot of new leads, which is what keeps your business growing. On the other hand, if your sales are all from new business, it could mean you are not giving good enough service to get customer repeats and referrals. It's important to keep track of these numbers.

Building a database is one of the most valuable things you can do as the CEO of your business because it is the only real asset you have. Build it consistently from the beginning. If you ever decide to sell your company, its value will be determined by the size of your database!

2. **Present yourself as successful—both in actions and appearance.** Once you are convinced that you are the CEO of your

own real estate business, you must present yourself as the CEO of a successful company to your market, or make sure that the way you conduct yourself is congruent with what you've presented as your brand. People want to do business with successful people. They want to validate their choice and one way you can help them do that is your everyday presentations through your clothes, your car, and your office. Steven Covey advises in his book, *The 7 Habits of Highly Effective People*, that you "begin with the end in mind." In other words, visualize what you want your business to look like from a branding perspective and then act and dress to present that image every day in every way.

3. **Choose a name with room to grow.** The name you give your business goes a long way toward presenting an image of success. If you're going to go to the highest level in this business, you are not going to be able to do it alone. So one of the things to consider is whether you want to present the perception that you are a lone ranger or a team. Using a name that signifies one person (such as just using your name by itself) presents the perception that you are alone in your efforts to serve your clients—and every client is going to expect to see *you* at his door. To avoid this perception, you may want to consider naming or renaming your business something that conveys that you are not alone—that you are a team or an entity, rather than an individual. If you use a generic name, or at least put the word "Group" after your own name (our business is named The McKissack Group), it lets the clients know that there is an entire team ready and willing to be of service to them, and any one of your team could represent your company.

As a Real Estate Agent, it is very important that you create a compelling presentation to deliver. Many of your competitors today still use the old sell-and-tell type presentation—telling the client how great they are, all about their accomplishments in the real estate business, etc. If you do that, you leave yourself wide open for challenge because the focus is on you. We have found that the best way to interact with a client is with what we call the *consultative-style presentation*—finding out all you can about your clients and focusing on them with questions like: what are their needs, what is important to them, how can you best serve them and meet and exceed their expectations, etc.

Another component of a compelling presentation for a real estate agent is moving people from emotion to logic. People don't make great decisions emotionally, so you must incorporate great logical questions in your presentation that move them from emotion to logic whether you are presenting to a seller or a buyer. Let's say you are selling a home for clients who have lived in their home for 20 years, and all of their children were raised there. They are probably very emotionally attached to their home. In order to move them to a place where they can make logical decisions about the listing price of their home, you might ask, "If you were the buyer, how much would you be willing to pay for this home?"

Start selling yourself to your customers as a successful person from day one. Believe it yourself, and then present yourself and your business with confidence. Look your clients in the eye and assure them that you are the person that can meet their real estate needs.

4. **Communicate your brand in everything you do, and be consistent.** In order for your brand to have the effect you want—to make your business "top of mind" to people in your market—you must communicate your brand in *everything* you do: your company logo, your business cards, your postcards, your newspaper ads, your marketing flyers, your vehicles, your billboards, your t-shirts, and anywhere else you have an opportunity to present it. In order to communicate the same message about your company in every piece, you must be consistent. Communicating your brand in some things

and not in others dilutes the presentation of your brand to your market and thus limits your opportunities for success.

5. **Be bold and different in communicating your brand.** We've done some crazy, fun things to present our brand to our market. In one ad, we used a picture of us on top of our house with the caption, "List your house with us, and we'll get right on it." Research tells us people are attracted to children and animals, so we use a lot of both. We did one ad in which we used a picture of us with an Irish setter, saying "Dependable and Trustworthy—and So Is the Dog." After a while, people told us they got to where they would open up the Sunday paper just to see what we had done that week. It has had an amazing effect on presenting our brand in our market.

6. **Tactfully drip—or touch—people often so they remember you.** Our research has shown, that we have to "drip" on people eight times before they will pick up the phone and call us. One "drip" could be that we sold their neighbor's house across the street, or that they saw our ad in the Sunday paper, or that they received a "sold card" from us in the mail. We put so many "drips" out there now that people find it hard to list just one thing when we ask them in their initial call what made them choose our company!

It is very important that you communicate your brand well through your marketing pieces. Be aware, though, that creativity can be one of the worst enemies of a new business owner. Don't spend so much time being creative that you can't focus on the things that really make you money. There are books out there that contain samples of marketing pieces that have worked well for other real estate agents. You can find them on the Internet or in the business section at any bookstore. One such book is Howard Brinton's, *A Marketing Scrapbook*, available at www.gostarpower.com. We suggest that you invest in such a book and find the pieces that work for you (only those that are not trademarked or copyrighted, of course). That's what we did when we were first beginning to market ourselves as a brand. It saved us untold hours of work, and we didn't have to re-invent the wheel.

7. **Choose a motto, or a theme, to use in your marketing.** Choose one that is consistent with your brand. Then be consistent with your theme and present it in everything you do along with your brand. That doesn't mean your motto can't change from time to time (although you don't want to change it too often or you will risk confusing your customers). In fact, we have had several different ones throughout our career. But whatever theme we have presented on a billboard, we have also presented on our postcards and everything else we do. Our current motto is "Families Helping Families," and that theme dovetails right in with our brand.

8. **Leverage your photo.** Everywhere we present our brand you see a picture of the two of us along with Jim's brother, Brad— a family.

Your picture is invaluable in presenting your brand as a real estate agent. It gives people the feeling that they know you and can trust you. Be sure to use a picture that is conservative and realistic— one that will make you seem approachable and will make people feel comfortable with you. We use our pictures to communicate our brand on our real estate signs, on our billboards, on our business cards, on our vehicles, on our stationery, on our postcards, in our newspaper ads—on everything we do. People tell us constantly that they see our picture everywhere. Or, like the man in the mall at the beginning of the chapter, they have seen us so much that they feel comfortable enough to approach us.

Once we attended our 13-year-old son's basketball game and stayed afterward to watch the girls' team from his school play. The girls' team defeated a team from a nearby town. As we were leaving, a complete stranger walked up to us and joked, "Well, folks from *that* town aren't going to be buying any houses from you!" This kind of thing no longer surprises us. In fact, we are always grateful when it happens because we know our brand is working for us.

9. **Reinforce your brand with good service and added value.** Everyone says they have "good service," but there are very few companies that make you feel at the end of the transaction that they truly cared about you and the results they got for you. To us, *standard* "good service" is meeting and exceeding the client's expectations, dealing with customers with integrity and in a timely and professional manner, and communicating with the client in the way that they choose and as often as they choose (by telephone once a week or by e-mail, etc.). Anything less is not good service. But we have always tried to go above and beyond and deliver *great* service.

Even beyond great service, there is any number of things you can do for your clients that adds that special touch that says "I care" and that will endear you to your clients. For example, Tony Jeary reads hundreds of self-improvement books a year and then summarizes them. Sometimes he sends these summaries out to clients via an e-blast, even if the book has nothing to do with his business. When clients come in to his Success Acceleration Studio, he may give them copies of two or three book summaries to take home with them. A lot of people love reading, and these book summaries provide a unique value add.

Remember that people give because they love to give, not to get something in return. But the magic thing that happens is, when people receive, they feel "beholden" to give something back. Tony calls this the principle of "reciprocation," and it is one of the methods of influence that he shares in his book *Life Is A Series Of Presentations.*

Tony's theory is that when someone does us a favor, we have an obligation to repay. He must be right because we have found that people want to be sure to use our services if we have done something "above and beyond" for them. They also want to tell all of their friends and family about their wise decision to hire the right agent who exceeded their expectations over and over again. Some of the added-value services we offer to our real estate clients are:

- Loaning our moving truck for local moves
- Allowing free use of our fax and copy machines and our in-house notary
- Sending out homestead exemption forms annually
- Holding customer appreciation parties
- Supplying free competitive and market-value information to our clients
- Providing data that will help home owners lower their taxes

We don't know that any one of these services is a compelling reason for our clients to do business with us. But we do know of several great benefits that providing added-value service brings to us:

- Added-value services continually keep our brand out in front of people. When our clients come to our office to use our copier or fax machine, they are going to see us. When they use our moving van—with our brand wrapped all around it—they (and a lot of other people) are going to see us.
- They give us a leg up over other real estate agents who don't offer the same services. Sometimes it's just that little edge that makes the crucial difference.
- They create loyalty to our brand. We have watched Tony continually give to other people. It's obvious that he loves to give, and so do we.

We also provide another added-value service to our clients that is quite unique. We have a referral-networking group of other professionals with whom we do business—a handyman, decorator, dentist, pediatrician, roofer, a home inspector, etc. When we do a closing, we give the new homeowners a notebook; on the inside of that notebook is a list of all the people that are in our networking group with their names and business phone numbers and addresses. Since we are dealing with people who are moving into a new community and are looking for those types of professionals, this notebook is an added-value service to our clients. It's also a great way for us to expand our brand because people in our networking group refer us to their friends and customers as well.

As a single agent, you may be able to deliver great service working alone, but as you grow you will have to leverage yourself in order to provide great service to your clients. *The three things that will allow you to really leverage yourself are:*

1. *Hiring great people* (see Chapter Ten)
2. *Building great systems* (which we will discuss throughout the book)
3. *Using great technology* (see Chapter Two)

People expect outstanding results from the service they get from us. They don't necessarily care who delivers that service to them; what they do care about is that our system is their solution. To deliver great service, you must put excellent systems in place.

There is one caveat in considering what added-value services to provide for your clients: It is easy to slip into the role of property manager or maid if you are not careful. When we first started in the business, we washed dishes before a showing and did anything else we thought would help the home sell. Obviously, we wore ourselves out doing things we were not hired to do, and that's NOT what we mean by added-value services. The real estate profession today has evolved into a much more professional industry—much like the medical or legal professions—but there are still many ways you can provide added-value services while maintaining your professionalism.

10. **Present that you are successful at the specific things your clients want to accomplish.** Sellers, for example, want three things: to get their homes sold for the top dollar in the shortest amount of time with the least amount of hassle. Once you get a successful track record, you want to announce as often and through as many media as possible, "We sold this many homes in less than so many days at over list price." Use statistics from the National Association of Realtors® (NAR) or your local association to validate your claims. We tell our clients, for example, that NAR statistics show that in the national real estate market homes are sold at 94 percent of list price, but our homes sell at 98 percent of list price. For a $200,000 home that difference equates to $8,000 dollars!

There are two reasons people take action. One is out of fear, and the other is for opportunity.

Tony coaches clients through the different factors that motivate audiences. One of those motivating factors is the perception of loss. Tony points out, "People seem to be more motivated by the thought of *losing* something than by the thought of gaining something of equal value."

In your consultative presentation, you can determine which motivation your client is acting from, and then tailor your presentation accordingly. One of your client's biggest fears may be that his house won't sell. When you share your successful track record with him about how many homes you sold in a short amount of time, his biggest fear may become that his house wouldn't sell if he went with someone else! If you have a great track record of selling at or above list price, your client will probably want to jump on the opportunity to list with you in order to get the best price.

An important thing to present to most sellers is that your company does the most marketing. There is an age-old misconception among sellers that advertising their homes is what sells their homes. But real estate agents know that advertising ourselves as a brand is what brings in the buyers—but not necessarily for the listing being advertised. So how do you make the seller happy but still do something that is effective? One of the things we do is advertise that we do the most advertising. And we do. We advertise ourselves as a brand more than any other agency in our market, and it brings in a steady stream of buyers.

To continually expand your brand, present a "call to action" in every marketing piece. This technique is simply another way to present your brand and get clients to call you. Tell your target market what you want them to do, and then make it easy for them to do it. For example, you might say, "Call us for a free computerized evaluation of your home," and include your phone number. (Make your phone number easy to remember—perhaps something like 555-848-MOVE.) If you send out marketing pieces that don't have a call to action, your prospects won't do anything, and you will never really know to what extent that piece has benefited you. With a call to action, you can measure the results and can almost guarantee a certain percentage of return. For every 50 postcards you send to people you haven't met, typically one will actually pick up the phone and call. When you send the cards to people you have met, the response rate generally improves to 12:2.

11. **Consistently present using third-party testimonials.** Help define your brand by making the most of what satisfied customers have said about you. Start getting testimonial letters from satisfied clients from the very first day you are in the business because these testimonials are valuable tools you can use in your marketing pieces. The best people to ask for a testimonial letter are those who have used your services, know you well, love you, and would never use anyone but you. But at the conclusion of every sale, we also send out a questionnaire (with a stamped envelope), asking the client to evaluate our services. At the bottom of the questionnaire, we ask if we may use their comments as a third-party testimonial. Third-party testimonials are a powerful way to add influence to your presentations. They provide social proof that your presentation is credible. They also invoke the principle of Liking. We have a tendency to be receptive to messages from people who like us and are like us.

So third-party testimonials give you two kinds of influence in one. The best time to ask for a reference, of course, is at the end of a successful transaction when the clients are happiest. After we sell a home, we send out 500 direct mail "sold cards" to the people who live around that particular home on which we include third-party testimonials. We have found these sold cards to be very effective because they validate our brand and get it in front of potential clients who may not have even considered selling their home up to that point. Here are examples of client testimonials and a sold card that we have used. You can find more examples of testimonials and sold cards at www.PresentationMasteryforRealtors.com.

"Absolutely professional to the T." — JOE KETCHUM

"Awesome—very knowledgeable, thorough and helpful. Never too pushy." — PATRICE BOWLES

"Excellent! Great Team!" — DS

"Very aggressive-very informative. Kept in contact reporting what was happening regarding the sale. Excellent!" — SANDRA COPP

12. **Present your brand to appeal to the different behavioral styles**. One of the eight presentation essentials we listed in the Introduction was "know your audience.' Knowing the basic wants, dislikes, personalities, and quirks of the person to whom you

are presenting adds significant effectiveness to your presentation. We use the DISC Profiler tool to determine information about our audience, from time to time, depending upon the situation and relevance. This assessment was originally developed in 1928 based on the work of psychologist William Moulton Marston and has been used for many years to determine personality behavioral profiles. More recently, a colleague of Tony's, Dr. Robert Rohm, developed a simpler diagram of the model to help determine a person's personality type.

In his book, Tony describes the four types as follows:

- The "D" type is outgoing and task-oriented. Company presidents, CEOs, and strong leaders usually have "D" personalities. They want to get to the bottom line of things in a hurry. "D" types don't want to be involved in long, touchy-feely conversations. They want to kill the cow, skin it, and eat it as quickly as possible. Obviously, if you are addressing a "D" personality, you don't want to waste a lot of time before getting to the core of your message.

- The "I" Type is outgoing and people oriented. These are the folks who love to talk and talk, and they've never met a person they don't like. "I" personalities tend to become salespeople, trainers, or speakers—or they enter other careers that afford them the opportunity to spend most of their time with people. "I" personalities want to feel good about themselves, and they don't want to hear a lot of bad news or too much detail. If you are addressing an "I" Type, you need to get him or her involved with you. Since they love to participate, they will gladly do anything you ask them to do in a group presentation . . . so long as it's fun and exciting.

- The "S" Type is reserved yet still people-oriented. These folks are sympathetic to the needs of others and have a high degree of empathy. Counselors and people who love to teach have "S" personalities. An "S" personality will gladly make sacrifices to help another person in need. If you suspect you are addressing a group of "S" personalities, let them know how they can help you. They'll be eager to do so.

- The "C" Type is reserved and task-oriented. These people want to know all the nitty-gritty details, and they are willing to spend as much time as it takes to get them. Accountants, auditors, and investigators have "C" personalities. If you are addressing a roomful of "C" Types, bring a lot of charts, graphs, and statistics. The "C" personality wants to know the tasks that lie ahead and each step necessary to accomplish those tasks.

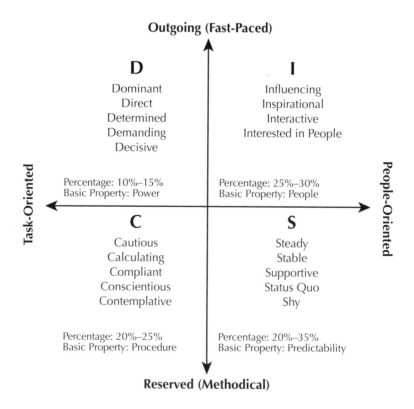

When a client calls our office, it is very important that the person answering the phone determine—through a series of questions—what type of personality that client has. (We have included in Chapter Four a copy of the forms our people use when answering the phone—one for a seller and one for a buyer. They are also available on www.PresentationMasteryForRealtors.com.) The agent who will be making the presentation must have that information in order to adequately prepare for his or her presentation to the client. What's important to a "D" personality is time, so a "D" personality client will want to know that you can sell his home quickly. He will want to know the bottom line right away and has a fear that you may take advantage of him. A high "I" personality is influenced by who has done business with you in the past. She will want to see testimonials. An "S" is more concerned about stability and security, so you may want to emphasize how long you have been in the business. She will want to know you have been around for a while and that you have a proven record. A high "C" personality is interested in being correct. Include statistics and a lot of data when presenting to him, and be prepared to leave him "homework" to read and analyze. High "Cs" are typically slow decision makers.

It's important to keep these personality types in mind when presenting your brand to your market and when presenting one-on-one as well. Include information in your marketing efforts that will appeal to each group. Remember, the more you know about the people you are presenting to, the better your presentations will be.

Push the presentation of your brand quickly, so you can grow big fast, *but be ready to provide the service that comes with fast growth.* Our growth in the real estate business in the beginning was long and slow. It took us a while to convert our real estate sales "job" into a real estate sales "business." We didn't have the money to properly market ourselves in the very beginning, nor did we have the knowledge. We did become a learning-based business early on, but we were slow in learning to present our brand well. While we found great outside training, we didn't have anyone giving us the "secrets to help us position our brand" to become successful. By applying the Presentation Mastery™ principles in this book, you *can* grow your business. In this business, how-ever, *if you don't build a foundation of great service with a great team at the same time as you are building your company, you won't reach the level of success you want to achieve.*

Within the last couple of years, two different real estate agents have come into our area that played out this sce-nario. They entered the marketplace and immediately pumped a lot of money into newspaper and magazine ads, color photos—the whole works. They did a *phenom-enal* job of presenting their brand. They invested a huge marketing budget from day one, even without knowing the kind of results they would get. They gained market share very quickly. They did such a wonderful job of presenting their brands to the market that within about 12 months, people in this area felt like they had been in business forever. The problem with both companies was that they didn't build their foundations to be able to deliver great service. Their motives for doing what they were doing were more about beating the largest team in town rather than being the best real estate agents they could be. Both were masterful at getting people to want to do business with them, and had they had the right Atti-tude—a great service mentality. Each of them could have stayed in business for a very long time. As it is, however, one has already gone out of business, and the other one has declining statistics. You can build as big a name as you want, but if you can't handle the clients your business is going to go away.

One of the top agents in our company is a great example of the totally opposite scenario. He's been in business for only four years, and he has a tremendous success story. He did what the other two didn't do. He went out and presented his brand and was masterful at attracting the business, but he simultaneously put in place the foundations and people to service his clients. He is now the #1 agent in our company with over $4.5 million in gross commission income last year.

Tony has developed a Branding Matrix™ to help his clients quickly identify the various elements of their brands, and we have adapted the form for real estate professionals. It's a great tool. Use what you have just read and take time to answer the questions on the Branding Matrix.™

See www.PresentationMasteryForRealtors.com for your free copy.

Branding Matrix

#	Element	Description		
1	**Brand Description**	What do I want people to think? What reputation do I want my brand to develop? What are clients buying?		
2	**Values**	Core Value & Characteristics to market and leverage		
3	**Business Priorities**	Parameters for operating in family and business life		
4	_____ **is**	Work ethic and approach to work and life		
5	_____ **is Not**	Characteristics do not describe you		
6	**Leverageable Uniqueness**	Unique attributes and abilities that are marketable		
7	**Packaging**	The value (tools, expertise, image, etc.) that is leverageable to the market		
8	**Visual Image**	Physical image/ appearance		
9	**Mission Stmt.**	What drives all decisions		
10	**Brand Power**	The "thrust" behind the brand		
11	**Tagline**	Benefit-driven, descriptive		
12	**Positioning**	Roles within the market(s)		

#	Element	Description		
13	**Business Motto**	Statement of business approach		
14	**What People Think Of You**	Your perception of your perception in the market		
15	**What People Are Missing**	Your beliefs on what prospects are misunderstanding about you		
16	**Attributes Prized in the Workplace**	Attributes you possess that the market values		
17	**Identify Your Passions**	Record those things you are passionate about		
18	**Top 4 Marketing Tools**	Top tools and tactics to leverage		
19	**Where Is My Audience/ Prospect?**	Who are those who can and will decide to pay for your service?		
20	**External Barriers**	Real world roadblocks		
21	**Internal Barriers**	Self-imposed roadblocks		

Note: A true professional should be absolutely clear who they are, what they stand for and of course how they can and should communicate this to the world. This matrix can act as a foundation to speed up the process.

VERY *Important* P O I N T S

1. Learn from and model others. Making the decision to be a learning-based business early on in our real estate career has turned out to be our best secret weapon.

2. Present yourself as successful—both in actions and appearance. Once you are convinced that you are the CEO of your own real estate business, you must present yourself as the CEO of a successful company to your market.

3. The name you give your business goes a long way toward presenting an image of success. You may want to consider naming—or renaming—your business something that conveys you are not alone—that you are a team or an entity rather than an individual.

4. Communicate your brand in everything you do and be consistent.

5. Be bold and different in communicating your brand.

6. Tactfully drip on—or touch—people often so they remember you. Research has shown that we have to drip on people eight times before they will pick up the phone and call us.

7. Choose a motto or theme to use in your marketing that is consistent with your brand. People will remember you.

8. Leverage your photo. Your picture is invaluable in presenting your brand.

9. Reinforce your brand with good service and added value. You can't go wrong with either one.

10. Present to your market that you are successful at the specific things your potential clients want to accomplish.

11. Consistently present using third-party testimonials. Other people can sell you better than you can sell yourself!

12. Present your brand to appeal to different behavioral styles. Remember the DISC concept and the varying personality types that shape the world.

Presenting
To Your Market

"Everything comes to him
who hustles while he waits."
THOMAS EDISON

We were taught that prospecting was one of the best ways to build our business and that prospecting was much less expensive than other methods. There are two sides to this story. So our entire office went through a telemarketer-training program and started prospecting over the phone. What I didn't know was that you can't do teleprospecting 24/7. Everyone in the office was miserable; we hated coming to work. It was definitely NOT fun! We were tired and discouraged and quickly approaching burnout when Jim looked over at me one day and asked, "What makes you think that prospecting is the only way to build this business? Do you think McDonald's calls all of its customers each day to ask them to come in and buy a hamburger?" A light bulb suddenly came on! "Of course not," I replied, jerking off my headset. The rest of our staff quickly followed suit. After spending countless hours, days, and months prospecting with cold calls and on the phone, we suddenly realized that this activity *alone* was not taking us where we wanted to go, and we immediately started working on a marketing plan. That moment was a turning point in our business!

If prospecting is you going to the client and marketing is the client coming to you, which way would *you* rather have it? Unless you're a very high "I" in the DISC Profile, you will probably agree that less prospecting and more marketing is better. *In reality, however, we discovered that the most successful real estate businesses are a healthy combination of both: marketing-based and prospecting-referral-enhanced.* In the beginning, most agents gear their businesses toward prospecting out of necessity. People don't just magically walk through their doors asking to buy a home. Agents have to physically go out and present to the prospects. Then once the business matures and starts making money, agents start investing it in marketing.

Prospecting or Marketing?

The most successful real estate businesses are a healthy balance of both.

When we first got into the business, we were $600,000 in debt and desperate to make it work. Prospecting was what we knew, so that's what we were doing—going out knocking on doors, making cold calls, calling prospects on the phone, and holding open houses (sometimes as many as four a weekend!). While it is true that prospecting is inexpensive and doesn't cost anything but time and that many people starting out in the business don't have the money to go out and start marketing, there are major problems inherent with relying on prospecting alone. For one, you only have so many hours in a day to prospect, and when you run out of time, you hit an achievement ceiling. Another problem is, once you stop prospecting, your business falls off. As we discovered, there is high burnout in prospecting. But a marketing-based/prospecting-referral-enhanced business can grow as big as you want it to grow. Then it becomes a fun and exciting adventure to watch your marketing plan fill in the gaps where prospecting leaves off!

It didn't take us long to realize that marketing our business would make our lives easier. So when we started making money, we started reinvesting that money into marketing and advertising. Obviously, if you have the money on the front end as well as the knowledge to put that money to work for you in a marketing plan, then you can grow a lot faster. We were lucky to also come across a couple of wonderful marketing coaches who really helped us improve our skills—Howard Brinton at www.gostarpower.com and Brian Buffini at www.buffiniandcompany.com. I highly recommend both of them for help with building your marketing skills and referrals.

How to Present Your Business through Prospecting

Today we have taken our business to the next level, and when we have people fly in for half-day sessions to talk about their own business, and how we can help them build it, we often focus on prospecting and what they could be doing differently. In these discovery sessions, we focus on transforming their vision of their real estate career from a job, into a business that builds wealth. We help them identify an exit strategy to move beyond the listing, sale, listing, thought process. We teach them to think beyond the next listing. If you're always looking for that next listing, you're always going to be holding down a job—or in other words, searching for ways to make money and provide for your family, versus creating a wealth building business that pays residual income on a long-term basis. Selling homes is the first step, of course, so we coach them through prospecting, and how that can increase sales.

It is important to understand that although marketing is the underlying basis for our growth, prospecting still remains a large part of our business. We have found that a real estate company *must* continually generate leads to survive. People who get into real estate may think they are in the sales business, but they are really in the lead-generation business first. Once you've done that, you're in the sales and service business. Those who do not know how to generate leads join teams, become staff people, or get out of the business. *In fact, the #1 one reason people get out of the real estate business is that they do not know how to generate leads.*

We want to keep that healthy balance of marketing and prospecting because it works. In order to do so, we have learned to become *"prospect-generating presentation machines."* In other words, we have identified as many prospect-generating sources as we can find and have mastered the art of presenting to each source.

Eleven Ways to Prospect for Success!

#1: FSBO
#2: Expired and withdrawn MLS Listings
#3: Sphere of Influence
#4: Open Houses
#5: Geographic farm
#6: Client appreciation parties
#7: Seminars
#8: Allied Resources
#9: Relocation Companies
#10: New home Builders
#11: IVR Systems

1. **For Sale by Owner (FSBO)**—We have taken much of our philosophy concerning FSBO listings from a great book by Jerry
Bresser called *List More, Sell More* as well as from our own experiences
over the years. Basically, our philosophy is this: For-Sale-by-Owner
sellers don't usually understand what they are losing by listing as
FSBO. They are typically only looking at the one benefit of saving
the commission. What they don't realize is that about 90 percent of
the homes that are on the market are listed with real estate agents,
so buyers who want to find something quickly (which most buyers
do) are generally going to go to that larger pool of choices rather
than to the smaller pool of 10 percent of the homes listed as FSBO.
Jerry Bresser suggests that you take an "in-harm's-way" approach
with FSBO sellers and explain the harm that can come to them by
not listing their home on the market with a real estate agent.

Jerry suggests that your presentation to a FSBO owner should
go something like this: "Basically, there are four kinds of people
who look at homes. The first kind is in a hurry to move. They have
a sense of urgency. They may have been transferred, or have already
sold their present home, or just want to make a quick decision.

The second kind is not in a hurry. They have no sense of urgency,
but they are serious buyers. They may be young people or other first
time buyers...proceeding cautiously. Or...they may be second or
third time buyers looking for a very special home.

The third kind is looking for a real bargain. Their idea is to save
the commission that goes to a real estate firm, or worse, they want
to find someone who is desperate to sell so they can buy the home
for thousands of dollars under fair market value.

The fourth kind will never buy. They can't afford to buy, or just
don't want to. But they enjoy looking at homes for a pastime."

Sellers who are inclined to go FSBO will generally list with a
real estate agent either before they list as FSBO (if the agent can
convince them that they are putting themselves "in harm's way") or

about four to six weeks after, but not in between. *It is very important that you build a relationship with the owners during that four-to-six-week period. Your whole focus should be relationship selling.* We **do not** advocate manipulating the owners by telling them you have a buyer because that is not servicing the client with integrity! During those four to six weeks, we usually drop off things they will actually need, such as a Seller's Disclosure Statement or helpful information on anything ranging from how to do an open house to how to make sure their buyers are pre-qualified. Statistics show that less than 20 percent of FSBO owners end up selling their homes themselves.

2. **Expired and Withdrawn MLS Listings**—Agents generally list their properties to expire near the end of the month, so toward the last five days of the month there will be a flurry of listings that have not sold during the listing period. Your presentation to the owners of these expired properties is very simple: "Hi, this is Jean Smith with the Jane Doe Realty Group. I notice your property just dropped off the multiple-listing service. Do you still plan to sell?" If they say yes, respond with, "Great! I specialize in properties that should have sold but didn't, and I'll be happy to drop by your home and help you determine why it didn't sell the first time. Would Monday be okay, or would the weekend be better?" If they say no, respond with, "Great! I specialize in properties that should have sold but didn't, and I would be happy to come by your home and explore with you why it didn't sell the first time in case you decide to put it back on the market in the future. Would Monday be okay, or would the weekend be better?" As Tony points out in his books, a "No" is simply a request for you to modify your proposal or change your delivery. Many of those owners with expired listings are frustrated with their agents because their homes didn't sell the first time, upset because their agents didn't communicate with them, and/or not really sure why their homes didn't sell. We don't get into a dialogue with them over the phone about why their homes didn't sell; we schedule an appointment to visit with them about it in person.

It is not unusual for these homeowners to be frustrated because they have received 30 calls from different real estate agents that day, each one asking to re-list their homes. If an owner seems irritated by that, we say, "I can understand, Mr. Seller, that you are frustrated that you have had so many calls. Of the people who have called, have any of them sold 30 properties (or 60—whatever your statistic might be) since your home was on the market?" You may have to drop in just a little "sell and tell" at that point. Or you may want to break the ice with something humorous like, "Well, that's all the more reason for me to get over there so they will stop calling." Or, "That's why you need to list with us, so your home will sell this time and you don't have to worry about getting 30 calls again."

Again, it's all about the presentation. You usually have just a few seconds to bond and make that connection. You want to make people feel comfortable. They will feel your confidence in your voice; but if you're intimidated, they will sense that as well. Be aware that confidence is one thing and arrogance is another! Most people relate better to someone who is humble but humorous.

3. **Sphere of Influence**—This category consists of the people involved in your "sphere" of life. It might be people at church, a social club, the gym, or a reading group or bible study. You may find that a lot of leads exist in this group just for the asking. But you have to ask! These are acquaintances who could possibly do business with you, but they are not your family, closest friends, or allies. (People who know you and love you and would *never* do business with anyone else.) The people in your sphere of influence may or may not do business with you, even though you may think you have a strong bond with them! This happens all the time in Real Estate.

Agents find that an acquaintance they thought would choose them has listed with another real estate agent. This is just a well-known job hazard that every good agent has faced! Don't be discouraged, when it happens to you.

There are some solutions that can help you be more proactive and get listings. We recommend that you put them on a "33 Touch Program." (We try to touch, or "drip on," our prospects anywhere from 24 to 33 times a year as a continual presentation of our brand. These touches may include our calendar, our newsletter, our sold postcards, and any number of our other marketing tools—different things that we drip on people throughout the year to help them keep us top of mind when they think of real estate.)

4. **Open Houses**—This is a great source of leads because many of the buyers who attend open houses have homes they need to sell. In one shot you can attract buyers AND sellers. Anytime you go where there is a stream of people in the real estate market place you stand a great chance of meeting someone with whom you will connect and who may list his home with you.

5. **Geographic Farm**—When you identify an area in which you would like to become the neighborhood real estate specialist, you need to first make sure there is at least a ten percent turnover of homes in the area to make it worthwhile. It would also help to have a high volume neighborhood with a large number of rooftops, and a sales price indicative of the average for the area. This means you'll be getting a lot of business, if things are going right, because a lot of people will be buying and selling homes. Begin presenting your brand to the people in this neighborhood by mailing cards, calling people on the phone, leaving door hangers, and doing any other thing you can think of to get your name and face in front of them. Before you know it, you will become the neighborhood real estate agent for that area.

6. **Client Appreciation Parties**—These relationship-building events never fail to generate great leads. From time to time, we throw a big party and invite all of our past clients and their families just to let them know how much we appreciate their business. We may rent a movie theater and show a family movie, or we may rent a civic center and throw a 50's party with a band, costumes, balloons, and free pictures with the bandleader. We have also held a conference for our clients, co-sponsored by a mortgage company, during which we taught an all-day life-achievement course developed by our company called "Quantum Leap." We always give special recognition to the people who have given us the most referrals during the past year. The last time we had a client appreciation party it generated six home sales!

7. **Seminars**—We generally do seminars through local colleges, and we teach such courses as "How to Buy Your First House," "How to Sell Your Home," or "How to Buy Investment Properties"—anything real estate related in which people may be interested. Again, it's just another way to present our brand and get us out in front of people who have an interest in buying or selling a home.

8. **Allied Resources**—This group is your faithful few—the people who know you, love you, and would never think of doing business with anyone but you. Look at your market like a big target with three circles. The large outside circle is the public—everyone in your market. You start by throwing your big marketing net out to the general public: sold postcards, television ads, newspaper ads, etc. Your first goal is to pull as many people as you can from the public into your next target, your sphere of influence.

Then you "drip" on those people on a regular basis with the hope of moving a handful from your sphere of influence into your "bulls eye"—your allied resources.

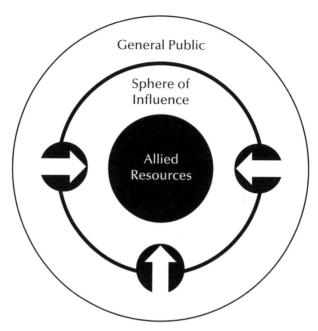

9. **Relocation Companies**—We have found that it is best to work with medium-sized companies who have relocation specialists in their human resource departments rather than working directly with relocation companies. Relocation companies can be difficult to work with. They have stringent requirements and large fees, and it has just not been worth the hassle for us. Getting to know the executives of medium-sized companies and working directly with them has always worked out better for us. Once you do a good job of taking care of their people, they refer you to executives of other companies.

10. **New Home Builders**—You will be dealing with one of two types of new home builders: custom builders or volume builders. We recommend that you find out who the custom builders are in your area and go out and build a relationship with them. It's important to know, however, that custom builders expect great service (as they should) and will move on to the next agent if you

don't give it. When I learned that a builder in our area had a bad experience with an agent, I went out to introduce myself and asked him to just let me show him what it would be like to work with me. I started filling his need, and before I knew it he had listed every one of his properties with me.

Working with volume builders is a little different. When you build a relationship with volume builders, you need to show them that you can help them move their products. One way we have done this is to provide a guaranteed sale. Basically, we provide a bridge for the new homebuyer who has a home to sell. We guarantee that we will buy their existing home for 95 percent of its value, plus a guaranteed sale fee, at the end of a predetermined listing period if the home has not sold. The builder writes our commission into his transaction for the new home. Our seller (the builder's new home buyer) can finalize the purchase of his new home with confidence, knowing his existing home will be sold, and the builder is guaranteed that the new home transaction will close. Not every agent can do this, and it won't always make sense to use this in your business or market. But it's an option that a lot of mega-agents use to build wealth.

All of our buying agents work with new homebuilders, and we have even made a "new home center" in our office where each builder has his own space to put floor plans and new home packets for our clients to review. Many agents are afraid to approach the builders because they have their own sales people, but we have found the builder's sales people to be great advocates for us. We encourage you to go out and build a relationship with these new home sales people and their district managers because they can be a great source of leads and can help you meet your buyers' needs. When you sell a new home through a builder, it will be one of the easiest sales you will ever make. The volume builders *want* you to bring your clients to their product, and they protect you on the sale. And the builder's sales people write up their own contracts and handle all the paperwork, making your job much easier.

Even if buyers say they don't want a new home, we believe that part of our job in working with them is to educate them on the whole market. The chances are that if we *don't* show them the new homes, they may decide they want one and go buy one without us! A fallacy that exists among buyers is that they get the house for less money through a builder if they don't go with an agent. The reality is that the price remains the same with or without an agent, and the agent provides representation for the buyer. Agents who have a great relationship with the builder and have already sold several houses for him may be able to negotiate a better deal on the home, and the agents are also there for the buyer in case there are any problems.

Another reason the builders love to see us coming with a client is that they know the client has been pre-qualified and that the preliminary work with that client has already been done. Many people look at new homes they can't afford to buy. But when they come out with a real estate agent, the builders know the buyers are serious about buying and are a triple-A prospect.

11. **IVR Systems**—This is the Interactive Voice Response System that we use for our ads. It is one of our largest sources for prospects because we have so many homes on the market. The ads contain an 800 number for the customer to call to get information on the home, which makes it possible to present the homes on the market 24 hours a day. The system keeps track of the times people call, and it is surprising how many call late at night when they finally have time to sit down and open the newspaper. The IVR system also captures the phone number of the person who is calling on that ad.

Let's say, for example, that we run a "talking ad" (IVR) in a local newspaper. When the client calls the 800 number, he would enter the code for that property that appeared in the ad and hear about all the features on that property. After he completes the call, the system notifies our buyer's agents' via pager, which shows the caller's telephone number and the four-digit code he entered. The buyer's agent looks at his list of properties and determines which property the client was calling about, and he immediately calls the client back. He introduces himself and says something like, "Someone at this number has just called on our property on XYZ Street, and as an added-value service, we just want to find out if there is any other information we can get for you on that property." We discovered that the best return on investment for that type of lead generation is to call the person back very quickly. At the beginning, we were waiting a day to call back, and we weren't getting any results. But we learned that when we called the people back quickly with a non-invasive informational call (unlike a telemarketing call), we got the best results. A great benefit of the IVR system is that it allows people to "raise their hand" before they enter the market, and we get to see that hand first.

We have found that there are two kinds of people in real estate: those who don't know how to get business but go out and do something anyway, and those who don't know how to get business and don't do anything. Neither one knows how when they first get in the business. But the difference between the two is that one of them goes out and overcomes his lack of knowledge, and the other gets stuck in his.

If you find prospecting difficult, let me make a recommendation. I have learned to do my hardest tasks earliest in the week when my business energy is the highest, and to do the hardest things first thing in the morning when I have the most physical energy. So if prospecting is difficult for you, do it early in the week and early in the morning. Prospecting is simply a numbers game, and your success depends on the number of people to whom you actually make presentations. You are looking for one "yes" within a lot of "no's." Remember this acronym: SWSWSWWN—Some will, some won't, so what, who's next?

Presenting Your Brand through Marketing

Marketing—bringing the prospect to you—is a fascinating adventure that requires ingenuity and imagination. Be bold and have fun with your marketing. I described in Chapter One some of the billboard and newspaper ads we have used, and it's usually the clever ones that people remember. If you are in a Southwest Airlines market area, you have probably been attracted to—and remember—their humorous billboard and television ads. One bold marketing tool that Tony uses is to strategically give away books he has authored to people he meets in the first class section of an airplane (that's how he met Zig Ziglar). Tony gives his books to CEO's and human resource people, and attendees at his seminars, as well as his coaching clients. Using creativity in your marketing helps make you top of mind in your market. You may not have a book to give away, but you might think of something else that could add value and showcase your brand, like a pen, calendar, or other distinctive marketing tool.

You want to leverage your marketing to your best advantage, and we believe the best way for you to do that is to market hard to get listings. You discover very quickly in real estate that the one thing you are shortest on besides money is time. There are too many things to do and too little time to do them and only a few will actually make you money. Let me ask you this: If you are working with buyers only, how many transactions could you do today? Two, at the most. In fact, you may spend three days with one buyer and a week with another. But if you have 10 listings and you work with two buyers today, how many transactions could you possibly do? The answer is 12. You can get a listing in an hour and a half and then put it in MLS, and all the other real estate agents in your area, including your own team, will immediately start helping you sell that property. While you're out working with your buyers, there is a possibility that all 10 of those listings could be sold by other agents. Listings are multi-transaction opportunities—the ultimate leverage!

If you design your marketing to present to sellers rather than buyers, the listings will attract the buyers. A newspaper ad that says, "Call me today. I'll be your great buyer's agent," would probably not generate any calls. But an ad that says, "Call me today. I'll get your home sold in ten days," does generate a lot of calls, and the buyers follow. Most real estate agents market toward buyers, but most *successful* agents focus on listing houses because they know if they get great listings, it automatically brings in great buyers. We highly recommend that you direct all of your marketing toward listings in order to better leverage your time.

In this business, there are only two ways to make money— volume or margin. You can either do a high volume with a lower margin or a high margin with a smaller volume. You need to decide whether you will market toward the large listings or the smaller ones, or both. We assessed our area and realized that we could not do enough transactions if we only specialized in big listings. We knew that the upper-end properties would take too long to sell and there were simply not enough of them. So we decided to go for high volume, and we built our strategy around presenting to the whole market, which includes all price ranges. The large houses bring in the large commissions but take much longer to sell, so the smaller homes are our real bread and butter. It takes the same amount of work for both, but one moves faster than the other.

We can't emphasize enough how important it is to set up systems from day one to track where your business comes from because this information tells you where to budget your marketing money for the next year. Why spend money on something that isn't working, and how will you know it's not working if you don't track your leads? When anyone calls our office, our staff is trained to ask that person what made them call our company.

We have already mentioned the Interactive Voice Response System that we use in our ads. Each ad has a four-digit code, and the codes vary for magazine and newspaper ads. The last digit of the code tells us where we placed the ad. When the client calls the 800 number in the ad and enters the code, it gives us a way to evaluate the effectiveness of that ad. It is a great lead-generating tool, plus it shows us what ads and publications are getting the best results.

Our postcard campaigns are also great lead-generating tools. We always include a call to action on our sold postcards. So when a client calls in to ask for the product advertised on the cards (a free market analysis of their home, for example), we know that lead was generated from the cards. All of these processes allow us to be the best fiduciary we can be to our clients because they help us gauge whether we need to advise the seller to go down on his price or the buyer to come up in his offer based on the number of leads we are getting.

We suggest that you design your marketing plan and stick to your plan as closely as possible for at least 12 months. The two main things you want to keep in mind, of course, are your budget and your return on investment. We usually design our plan in November for the following year. Sometimes it can take 90 to 180 days before a campaign even starts to work, depending on the group to whom you are marketing. If you are presenting to people who know you (like your past clients or your allied resources), they respond differently than people who don't know you.

When you are designing your marketing strategy, you need to think long-term but be responsive to short-term. Don't expect immediate results from every marketing piece you use. Different pieces will take different amounts of time to be effective. Some will give you name recognition, and others will cause people to take action immediately. If you don't include a call to action on the marketing piece, it will be strictly institutional—something that builds your brand but does not give you immediate results. With institutional marketing, it is difficult to know what results you are getting, other than asking clients why they chose to call you.

If you find that something is not working, pull it quickly and switch to a different strategy. The advantage a real estate company has over a large corporation is that we can pull something and switch gears relatively quickly, whereas a large company generally has so many administrative layers to go through that they are not able to make quick changes even if they have millions of dollars invested in a marketing plan that isn't working. Several years ago we made over 100,000 color postcards with our son's adorable face on the front. (We use children and animals a lot in our marketing pieces because we have discovered that is what people like to see.) They were the most beautiful cards you have ever seen, but we had failed to include a call to action on the card, and we found out rather quickly that they were just not effective. We spent a lot of money on that piece, but we had no choice but to scrap it. Now, to throw away that many marketing pieces is one thing, but as every mother knows, to throw away that many with your child's face on it is another! (There's a reason those photographers give you those pictures to take home. . . .) But we knew we had to respond quickly, and we did. It's important to hold each piece accountable in order to get the return-on-investment results you want. If it's not working, change it.

Our years of experience and success in marketing our real estate business have taught us what works and what doesn't, and we have identified 13 marketing tools that give us the highest impact in presenting our brand to our market.

1. Billboards on major interstate highways (with our picture)
2. Calendars
3. Commercial items (pens, children's coloring books, magnets, t-shirts, etc.)
4. Moving trucks
5. Newsletters
6. Newspaper ads (marketing toward sellers)
7. Postcard campaigns (sold cards)
8. Real estate magazine ads
9. Real estate signs (with our picture)
10. Television ads
11. Vehicle signs
12. Websites (see Chapter Three for how to build a great website)
13. Yellow page ads

Marketing is an in-depth process, however, and our overall presentation/marketing collateral is much more exhaustive. We have included a Presentation/Marketing Collateral Audit—a categorized list of 63 presentation and marketing tools—so you can assess your own marketing collateral to see if you are presenting your brand for the highest impact. This audit is a great planning tool to use when you are developing your Strategic Business Plan.

Presentation/Marketing Collateral Audit

Company Name: **Date:**

#	Collateral Item (What)	Purpose (Why)	Action (How)	Budget
Foundations for your Marketing Identity				
1.	Branding Matrix			
2.	Strategic Business Plan			
3.	Logo*			
4.	Value Proposition or Unique Selling Position (USP)			
5.	Slogan/Jingle/Tagline*			
6.	Color Scheme*			
7.	Customer Focus			
8.	Organization's Profile			
Basic Graphic Identity Materials—Signage				
9.	Exterior Signs			
10.	Vehicle Identification			
11.	Interior Signs			
12.	Foam Board			
Basic Marketing Identity Materials—Paper				
13.	Stationery: Letterhead, Envelopes and Mailing Labels*			
14.	Fax Cover Sheet			
15.	Business Cards*			
16.	Brochure(s)*			
17.	One sheets*			
18.	Press Kit			
19.	Newsletter			
20.	Business Reply Card			
21.	Direct Mail Pieces			
22.	Catalogs			
23.	Stationery: Thank You Cards			
24.	Personalized Index Cards			
25.	Forms			

Company Name: **Date:**

#	Collateral Item (What)	Purpose (Why)	Action (How)	Budget
26.	Self-Inking Stamps / Labels			
27.	Tent Cards			
28.	Biography(ies)*			
29.	Pitch Book			
30.	Statement Stuffers			
Marketing Identity Elements in Electronic Media				
31.	Website			
32.	E-mail Stationery (electronic letterhead)			
33.	PowerPoint Message			
34.	Video Brochures*			
35.	Video Brochure Covers			
36.	Audio Business Cards— Brochures			
37.	Telephone System Messages— On Hold and Voice Mail			
38.	Software / Software Inserts			
39.	Media-Ready CD			
Market Information (Sales, Customer and Prospect)				
40.	Database			
41.	Database Software			
42.	Case Studies			
Resources and Archives				
43.	Photo Library			
44.	References/Testimonial Letters			
45.	Trade Show Materials			
46.	Desk Trinkets			
47.	Luggage Tags			
48.	T-shirts			
49.	Hats			
50.	Posters			
51.	Banners and Signs			
52.	Bumper Stickers			

Company Name: **Date:**

#	Collateral Item (What)	Purpose (Why)	Action (How)	Budget
53.	Calendars			
54.	Envelope Teaser			
55.	Coupons/Tickets			
56.	Door Hangers			
57.	Point of Purchase Materials			
58.	Card Decks			
59.	Newspaper Inserts			
60.	Advertisement Templates (Icons)			
Special Actions and Activities				
61.	Awards Received			
62.	Awards Sponsored			
63.	Contests & Events Created			
64.	Contests & Events Sponsored			
65.	Celebrity Sponsor/Spokesperson			
Public, Press and Community Relations Activities				
66.	Articles and Columns Written			
67.	Organizations and Affiliations			
68.	Organizations Started			
69.	Community Involvement			
70.	Marketing with Celebrities			
71.	Media Releases			
72.	Feature Stories			
73.	Guest on Talk Show or Radio			
Institutional Advertising				
74.	Classified Ads			
75.	Yellow Pages			
Publishing				
76.	Trophy Book			
77.	Handbook			
78.	Passport Book			
79.	White Paper			
80.	CD/DVD			

Company Name: **Date:**

#	Collateral Item (What)	Purpose (Why)	Action (How)	Budget
	Presentation Materials			
81.	Action Cards			
82.	Notetakers/Handouts			
83.	Coined Phrases			
84.	Coaching Cards			
85.	Bio Cards			
86.	Evaluations			
87.	Special-Titled Processes			
88.	Pre-Session Survey			
89.	Event Check List			
90.	Signatures (dollar bill pads)			
91.	Follow-up			

The Foundation for Building Your Business

1. Branding Matrix—Building your brand is the first step towards building your foundation, from which to market. We discussed the Matrix in Chapter One, and a sample Branding Matrix is included on pages 28–29.

2. Strategic Business Plan—Even though a business plan is a strategic tool, we have found that few real estate agents ever do one. We usually do our business plan in October for the next year. It is based on the number of units we want to sell for the year, rather than on volume. Units are duplicatable; volume is not. We may have sold a million-dollar home once, but realistically we may not be able to do that every year, and we don't build our business plan on that possibility. We do continually strive to move our average sales price up each year, however. Our business plan is not something we do once a year and then put it in a drawer and forget about it. We are

constantly looking at this plan—at least weekly—so we can make adjustments to our strategy as needed. You can find examples of business plans on the Internet and in the business section of bookstores and libraries.

3. **Logo**—If you don't have a logo, you need to create one because it plays a huge role in presenting your brand. Remember to follow your color scheme and be consistent with other marketing tools you have designed. We suggest that you use a picture in your logo that presents a professional image because that goes a long way toward presenting your brand.

4. **Value Proposition or Unique Selling Position (USP)** —In the real estate business, we know that the three things a seller wants is the highest price for his home in the shortest amount of time with the least amount of hassle. We gear our marketing towards these things, and we communicate to our sellers that those are the benefits they will get when they work with us. That proposition is our unique selling position (USP). The USP never changes. It is unique to our business and is the selling proposition that makes clients want to do business with us. At every opportunity, we present that proposition to the public by telling them about the homes we sell very quickly for the listing price or above.

5. **Slogan/Jingle/Tagline**—Make sure that your slogan, jingle (if you have one), and tagline all identify with your logo or your USP. Our logo is a picture of the McKissack family—Brad, Jim, and myself—and our slogan is "Families Helping Families."

6. **Color Scheme**—Be sure to test your color scheme in print and on your website to see how it is going to look. Some colors look better in one medium than the other, and some colors have a more positive effect than others. Be consistent (even in the clothes you wear in your picture), and make certain that your color scheme makes good,

solid sense rather than just using the colors you like. Then tie every-thing together with your color scheme—your logo, your signs, your business cards, your vehicle signs, your billboards, etc. The idea is to burn a total image of your brand—including colors, pictures, and messages—into the minds of the people to whom you are market-ing, so there will be an immediate connection with you even if they just see your colors. A friend told me that a hotel chain used to have the same color scheme as a popular food company in the southwest, and she could never see their sign without thinking of ranch style beans. (They have now changed their color scheme. Could it be that others conjured up the same picture when they saw their sign?)

7. **Customer Focus**—The very foundation of your business is your customers. Always focus on what is important to them—what benefits you can provide to your customers. When customer focus becomes part of your brand, your business will increase dramatically.

8. **Organization's Profile**—Who are you as an organization? Who are your people? How do you want to be known? We are, as our slogan says, "Families Helping families." We are known as a learning-based family organization. It's not unusual for people calling in to assume that all of our agents are part of the McKissack family.

Marketing Your Business

9. **Exterior Signs**—We use yard signs, directional signs, billboard signs, vehicle signs, and a sign on our moving truck. They all fit into our color scheme, they all have our pictures on them, and they all have the name of our company and our phone number on them. It's a continual presentation of our faces and our name!

10. **Vehicle Identification**—We don't just put signs *on* our vehicles. We *wrap* our vehicles in our signs. People definitely know it's the

McKissack Group coming when they see our Hummer! It's a great way to present our brand.

Basic Marketing Identity Materials—Paper

13. Stationery: Letterhead, Envelopes, and Mailing Labels—Again, include your logo (which should include your picture) and be consistent with your color scheme. It's very important that you make the same presentation of your brand on all of your paper marketing identity materials. The appearance and message of each piece should make it immediately identifiable with the rest of the "family" pieces.

14. Fax Cover Sheet—Just as with your stationery, your fax cover sheet should include the same presentation of your brand.

15. Business Cards—While your business cards do not have to include all of the elements on your stationery, you should ensure that the presentation of your brand is consistent with the rest of the family pieces.

16. Brochure(s)—Many real estate agents don't use a brochure. If you do use one, make sure it looks very professional, that it is easily identifiable with the rest of your family of marketing tools, and that it provides a good return on investment. A great source for brochures is a company called Hobbs Herder out of Newport Beach, CA. They are real estate specific, and they do a great job.

17. One Sheets—The information sheets that you put both inside and outside of a home you have listed should also be consistent in the presentation of your brand message and image.

15. Pre-Listing Packets—The folders you use for your pre-listing packets can be great multi-faceted marketing tools. We print legal-sized folders with our brand (name, picture, logo, slogan, web site, phone numbers, etc.) on the front cover. Then on the inside and back covers we print small ads for each person in our networking group, including a new home builder, an appraiser, a mortgage company, a home inspection company, an insurance agent, a bank, a dentist, a roofing company, etc. This information is helpful for the seller, and it is reciprocal marketing for our networking group. We also include a moving "to-do" list for the seller on the inside. Then we place inside the folder a booklet called *So You're Thinking of Selling Your Home*, which gives detailed information about our company, our staff (and how they can help the seller), the disadvantages of listing For Sale by Owner, and information about price and showing condition. We also include in the folder information about feedback (the purpose of it and how to access it on www. ehomeshowings.com), a brochure explaining our guaranteed sale program, a personal profile form to complete, a pre-qualification application with a local mortgage company, telephone numbers for all of the utility companies in our market (by area), a Seller's Disclosure Statement, information about brokerage services, brochures for various home warranty companies, and a Sellers' Estimated Charges form. The idea of course is to be customer focused—as attentive to the needs of our clients as possible.

19. Newsletter—Sending out a monthly newsletter to your client database goes a long way toward keeping your business top of mind in your community. Again, be sure to present your brand consistently. This is your chance to provide potential buyers and sellers with valuable information, and it doesn't have to be centered on homes! Some agents put local information, helpful hints, recipes, property tax information, and even random lifestyle articles in their newsletters.

20. Business Reply Card—We use these cards for out-of-town owners. We buy from the appraisal district a list of all the people who own

property in our area but have an out-of-town address. We send those people a postcard asking if they want to sell or lease their property, or if they need someone to manage it for them. We make it easy for them by asking them to check off the item on which they would like more information. The postcard has a business reply card on one end of it that they can tear off and mail back to us. Of course the post cards have our branding information consistent with the other pieces.

21. **Direct Mail Pieces**—We send out 250 "sold" cards to the people who live around each property that we sell, and we always include a call to action on these cards (like "Call me now for a free computerized evaluation of your home."). These cards always match our marketing theme and often include testimonials.

23. **Stationery: Thank-You Cards**—Thank-you cards should have your logo on them to match your other pieces. The goal in our office is for each of our agents to hand write at least six thank-you cards a day to anyone with whom they have been in contact that has been helpful to them.

25. **Forms**—If you send a survey form to your clients after each closing, it is best to have your logo on the form just like your other marketing materials. Many other real estate companies are now asking for copies of our internal forms, and this is another way to promote our brand since we put our name and logo on them.

Marketing Identity Elements—Electronic Media

31. **Website**—A website is essential for your real estate business, and you want to ensure that you present your brand consistently in this important medium. In Chapter Three, we provide in-depth information on using your website to market your business.

- **Virtual Tours**—These are relatively standard marketing tools for real estate agents in today's market, but don't forget to include your branding information just as you do on the rest of your website.

- **Technology**—Two things that support all of these kinds of marketing—and every aspect of your business—are your database and the software that runs it. We have about 4,200 prospects in our database. The database is really the only tangible asset that a service business has to sell, so you need to start developing your database from day one!

  There are numerous real estate database software packages on the market. We use Online Agent (now called Agent Office (www.realestate.fnis.com) for our database software, but another excellent application is called Top Producer (www.topproducer.com). We also use ShowingDesk (www.showing-time.com, formerly called CallTrax) that helps us keep up with all of our leads. Arch Telecom (www.archtelecom.com) is our 800 IVR system that captures the telephone numbers of call-in prospects.

32. E-Mail Stationery (electronic letterhead)—An electronic signature on your e-mails help further promote your brand.

33. PowerPoint Presentation—Some real estate agents use Power-Point presentations when they meet with a client. If you do something like that, make sure the frame of each page includes your company name and logo. Don't miss an opportunity to present your brand!

36. Audio Business Cards and Brochures—These are getting to be popular marketing tools among real estate agents. Rather than spending the money to print cards and brochures, you can burn the information on a CD that you can give to clients. You can also include more information on a CD than you can on a brochure.

37. **Telephone System Messages**—When our staff people answer the phone, they say, "It's a great day at the McKissack Group! How may we help you?. . .It would be my pleasure." as a way of promoting our brand. Many agents also use on-hold and voice-mail messages for a greater impact.

Market Information (Sales, Customer Support and Prospect)

42. **Case Studies**—It's very important for real estate agents to have an arsenal of stories that they can use when dealing with various circumstances. Let's say for example you get an offer on someone's home really quickly. Sellers often don't want to take the first offer, especially if it comes soon after they put their home on the market. If you have a real-life story about another client who refused the first offer and regretted it later, you can tell them, "You know, Mr. and Mrs. Jones didn't take their first offer either because they—like you—felt that if the first one was that good, the second one would be even better. But six months down the road, they took five percent (or ten percent, whatever the case was) less than their original offer." Those stories are valuable knowledge that will help you be a good fiduciary for your client.

Resources and Archives for Growing Your Business

43. **Photo Library (Scrapbook)**—It's important to capture—through pictures, articles, and mementos—the important events in the life of your real estate business: community events, marketing campaigns, client parties, etc. Your scrapbook documents your progress toward building your brand and is a great marketing tool when it's placed in your reception area for potential clients and visitors to browse through.

44. References/Testimonial Letters—Help define your brand by making the most of what satisfied customers have said about you. We recommend that you start getting testimonial letters from satisfied clients from the very first day you are in the business because they are valuable tools that you can use in your marketing pieces.

Resources and Archives

45. Trade Show/Convention Materials—When you have a booth at a real estate convention, hand out things to the other agents that will help them think of you when they make referrals to their clients who are moving to your area. We have given out things like rolodex cards that contain our contact information and lanyards with our logo on the front (for holding driver's license or other forms of I.D., convention tickets, etc.).

48. T-shirts—T-shirts are usually pretty popular, especially with children, so they can be very effective in presenting your brand. At one time our slogan was "Our System is Your Solution." We gave t-shirts to our sellers that said "Their System was Our Solution," and they had a big "Sold" sign on them.

49. Hats—Hats with your logo on the front are popular as well and help push your brand.

51. Banners and Signs—These are great for local marketing events in your community. We often have booths at local events where we do free market analyses for people.

53. Calendars—We have been sending out calendars for years, and they work *very* well for us. We use Melco Marketing out of Manassas, Virginia, and have had great service from them. Our calendars are on letter size paper (one page per month), and they fit into a

vinyl sleeve with magnets on the back and our branding information on the front. Each month has a big, red-letter reminder to call us for their real estate needs or to refer us to their family and friends. Our clients love these and start calling us in October to remind us to send them a calendar—two, in fact. . .one for their home and one for their office! Our calendars present our brand on a daily basis!

56. **Door Hangers**—This piece is a great marketing tool for new agents who want to become the real estate specialist for a certain area (geographic farm). Make sure the pieces are consistent with presenting your brand and include a call to action.

57. **Point of Purchase Materials (Closing Gifts)**—We give notebooks with our branding information on them to our clients at closing, so they will have something in which to keep all their closing papers. In the past, we have given ceramic cookie jar houses and t-shirts.

- **Pens**—People keep pens until they run out of ink. They are very cost effective in presenting your brand on a daily basis.
- **Children's Coloring Books**—We have had coloring books made that are all about families who are moving. These books are great promotional items to hand out at local community events. Anytime you do something for the kids the parents love you!
- **Measuring Tapes**—The guys love these items. Put your name and logo on the front.
- **Business Card Magnets**—Magnets are a very popular item, and many customers put them on their refrigerators—a great daily reminder that we are their real estate agents!

59. **Newspaper Inserts and Display Ads**—Since we don't live in a large metropolitan area with large-metropolitan-area-newspaper-

advertising prices, it is both affordable and productive for us to run full-page ads on the back page of our local newspaper three weeks out of every month. The results are phenomenal in the presentation of our brand. We recommend advertising in your local paper as much as you can afford it.

Special Actions and Activities

61. **Awards Received**—This is another great way to keep your name out before the public. Publicizing awards in the News Brief section of your local paper is an economical way to keep your name in front of the public. It also has the added benefit of increasing your credibility by showing that others value your efforts.

63. **Contests and Events**—We had a great contest a few years ago with our existing clients. Understanding that a verbal referral to a friend or family member sometimes gets "lost on the way to the phone," we taught our clients to call *us* with that person's name and number, so we could increase the odds of getting that referral. Then, whether the referral ever materialized into a listing or not, we recognized that client publicly. We sent balloons to their home or work with a thank-you note and a movie or restaurant gift card. It worked! It taught our clients to call *us* with a referral rather than just telling their friends or family to call us. Be creative and community-minded. A few years ago, we sponsored a coloring event that garnered a lot of attention. Sponsoring or holding events is a fun way to keep your brand in front of the public.

Public, Press, and Community Relations Activites

66. **Articles and Columns Written**—Newspapers are always looking for people with expertise in certain fields to write columns or articles.

Writing a column or article is a great way to present your brand to your community. Don't worry if you're not an accomplished writer. A good editor can quickly smooth out your copy.

67. **Organizations and Affiliations**—Memberships in professional organizations give credence to your business and keep you educated on important issues, especially the national and local real estate associations. We also belong to the Certified Residential Specialists, which is a great organization.

69. **Community Involvement**—Being involved in your community has a double benefit. Your community benefits from your actions and your business benefits from the presentation of your brand. On National Tree Day, we dedicate a tree to a local school. We go out to the school and plant the tree; then we give all of the teachers and students a small tree to take home. We also sponsor children's sports events.

71. **Media Releases**

- **Television Ads**—Many agents don't consider television ads because they think it is too expensive. However, we've found advertising through our local cable company to be a very successful, cost-effective way to advertise.

- **Billboards**—Although billboards can seem a little pricey, they more than deliver their return on investment. We ran a billboard advertisement along the major highway through our town. Although it's been over a year since the advertisement was taken down, people still comment on it and think that it is still being displayed!

- **Real Estate Magazines**—Advertising in real estate magazines can be very effective, but we've found it pays to do some research and find out which ones work best in your area. What works in one area may not necessarily work in another. Remember if it's not working, change it.

72. **Feature Stories**—These are great brand boosters! We have been featured in national, regional and industry magazines. Any time you can use your powers of persuasion (or those of a contact) to arrange for a feature story, your brand moves up a notch or two, especially if it's in a national publication.

Institutional Advertising

74. **Classified Ads**—These little three-line ads are not the most successful things we do, but they are certainly important. Buyers who don't have an agent often rely on the classifieds as a primary tool to identify properties for sale.

75. **Yellow Pages**—Many people look in the Yellow Pages for a real estate agent, so we put a lot of credence to advertising there. We usually carry a ⅛-page ad—large enough to be noticed.

Publishing

76. **Trophy (Informational) Books**—People seemed to be starved for knowledge today, and information books usually sell very well. People like me would rather pay $29.95 for a how-to book than try to re-invent the wheel. These books are not only a great way to promote your brand, but they are a great source of second income as well.

Value Added Services to Elevate You Above the Competition

1. **Moving Truck**—Our clients love the convenience and savings of using our moving truck, and people see our brand every time it goes out into the community.

2. **Assistance in Getting Property Tax Value Lowered**—Most people don't realize that there are numerous reasons their property tax may be calculated incorrectly. As an added-value service we will help present your case to the city/county officials to try to get your property tax value lowered.

3. **Automatic Mailing of Settlement Statement at Tax Time**—When tax season rolls around, clients who have closed on a new home need a copy of their settlement statements from their closing. Rather than waiting for them to call us to request a copy, we automatically send these out each year right before tax time, and our clients are delighted.

4. **Automatic Mailing of Homestead Exemption Form**—We send these forms out each year to those clients who qualify for the Homestead Exemption in our state (the first January they are living in their home). Since they will realize a savings of hundreds of tax dollars each year by filing for this exemption, they are very grateful for the reminder and the convenience.

5. **Free Competitive And Market-Value Information**—Whether or not a seller decides to list his property with us, we will do a free market analysis for him that shows the competitive value of his home in relation to others in the market. We will also do this even if someone isn't thinking of selling his home but just needs a market-value assessment.

6. **Free Notary Service**—Sometimes it's the little things that mean so much to our clients. They love the comfort of knowing this service is available when they need it.

7. **Free Use of Copier/Fax**—Access to our copier/fax machine is a great benefit to our clients, which translates into great promotion of our brand!

8. **Client Appreciation Parties**—These are great relationship-building events, and our clients are always looking forward to the next one. The parties often become the talk of the community, which is a great way to build our brand.

9. **Seminars for Clients**—We have given clients free tickets to our "How to Buy Investment Property" seminar and our "Life Achievement" course. Both courses have been an effective tool in promoting our brand.

VERY *Important* P O I N T S

1. The most successful real estate businesses are a healthy combination of both marketing and prospecting. They are marketing-based and prospecting-referral-enhanced.

2. The #1 reason people get out of the real estate business is that they do not know how to generate leads.

3. In order to keep a healthy balance between prospecting and marketing, you have to learn to become a prospect-generating presentation machine.

4. Your whole focus should be on relationship selling. Make people feel comfortable. You usually have just a few seconds to bond and make that connection.

5. Even if buyers say they don't want a brand-new home, part of your job in working with them is to educate them on the whole market.

6. Do your hardest tasks earliest in the week when your business energy is the highest, and do the hardest things first thing in the morning when you have the most physical energy.

7. You want to leverage your marketing to your best advantage, and the best way for a real estate agent to do that is to present his market toward listings.

8. It is very important to set up systems from day one to track where your business comes from because this information tells you where to budget your marketing money for the next year.

3

Presenting
on the Web

When Internet marketing began to take off, most real estate professionals feared the Internet because they thought it might replace them. Companies were popping up everywhere, asking agents to put their listings on their internet websites. Some turned out to be friends, and some foes. It was a very confusing time. We wondered if the consumer would be able to go straight to the Internet and never need a real estate agent again.

Since that time we have come to realize that people do *indeed* use the Internet to meet their real estate needs, but only as a functional tool to look for homes. Then they go to the agents who guide them through the process and serve as their fiduciary. *It is the public, in fact, that has demanded that real estate agents have a presence on the web because they use our sites as informational tools.* We are finding that most of our customers have already gone to the web and looked at homes before they ever get to us. So in many ways, the web has made our jobs easier!

In today's market the real estate professional that wants to rise to the highest level has several compelling reasons for presenting to their market on the web:

1. It gives you more exposure for your brand. *Building your website to clearly reflect your brand will make it one of the most powerful tools in your marketing arsenal.*

2. It is an incredible lead-generating tool. *About 40 percent of our leads come from our website now, compared to 10 percent a few years back.* In places like the Silicon Valley, the numbers are even higher.

3. It's what customers demand. They view it as an essential informational tool.

4. It is a great listing tool. Sellers are very happy to see their listings advertised on yet another venue.

5. It is an effective way to advertise homes. *It is much less expensive—and much more effective—to advertise homes on a website than it is to advertise in the newspaper.* If you're concerned about the cost of maintaining a web presence, remember that the savings over traditional marketing can be significant—not to mention the fact that you can include pictures, virtual tours, and much more information about each home on the web than you can in a small, expensive newspaper ad.

6. It's time efficient. You can market homes 24/7, and consumers can view the listings when it's convenient for them.

7. It's a global tool. People who are relocating from any country in the world can get on the web and look up homes in the area to which they are moving.

8. It's a time saver. Customers can narrow their choice of homes before they ever get to you.

9. It's the sign of the times. Each year, consumers are turning more and more to the web to find what they want.

The number of leads we get through the Internet has risen drastically over the past three or four years. Initially, though, the hardest thing about becoming an effective presence on the web was figuring out how to get customers to go to our website. *We quickly realized that it was very important to plaster our web address on everything we did—newspaper advertising, television advertising, billboards, sold cards, business cards, etc. We knew it would need to appear everywhere people looked—as a part of our brand—to drive people to our site.* We even put large banners in the newspaper with nothing but our website on them!

We also realized that, *to effectively drive traffic to our site, we needed to make sure we were listed with the best search engines to ensure that our name would be among the top results when people are searching for a home in our area.* We found a company called Number 1 Expert (www.number1expert.com), whose host company is Best Image. They do a great job of getting us listed with the top search engines, so our name comes up when people do a search for homes in the Denton County area. We cannot stress enough how important it is to choose a host company that will do that for you. We pay about $300 a month to our web host, and there was an up-front investment of about $5,000 to build the site, but it is one of the best investments we have ever made. Other than our own listings, which we change daily, and other information pertaining directly to our company, Best Image maintains our entire site and provides invaluable resources for our customers (market condition reports, access to national real estate newsletters, a Java-based mortgage calculator, and virtually all of the other resources we list on our site).

Four or five years ago, before we found Best Image, we used a different web-hosting company, and we only had the capability of showing outside views of the homes. We were told that we were getting thousands of hits on our listings, but we weren't getting the leads. Then we switched to Number 1 Expert, where customers can log in and see pictures of the different rooms inside the home as well as various views of the outside. Customers like to see a lot of pictures. So now we are not only making our customers happier by giving them more information about the homes, but we are able to capture contact leads from the login information. Yes, we get some leads with bogus information, but about 90 percent of the leads are good.

We have discovered another very effective tool for driving people to our site. We have purchased several domains with catchy names that attract customers, and we advertise them everywhere. For example, we put WhatIsMyHomeWorthNow.com on our sold cards, and this domain leads customers directly to a page on our site that has a form they can fill out for a free online market analysis of their homes.

We purchase banners in the newspaper to advertise:

- FreeMortgagePre-Qualify.com
- GuaranteeHomeSaleFast.com
- TopCashForHome.com
- WhatDidThatHomeSellFor.com

Each domain leads customers to a corresponding page on our website where they can fill out a form and get the information they are requesting.

REALTOR.com is another great ally in driving people to our website. When customers click on our listings on the REALTOR.com site, it leads them to our site. Paying their extra fee to include our name and logo with the listing is well worth the money.

Your website, of course, should be consistent with all of your other marketing tools as far as colors, logo, pictures, slogan, etc. A large part of our brand is being a family and community-based business, and we have built our website (www.mckissackrealty.com) around that theme. On the top left corner of each page there are pictures of the courthouse on our downtown square, a family park that was built by families in our community, and the beautiful countryside in our area. Our picture (Jim, Brad, and myself—the McKissack family) is on each page as well—just as it is on all of our marketing tools.

Although it is vital that your website present your brand in its overall look, remember that the main reason your customers go to your site is for information—period. They don't want a lot of personal information about you—they want to see homes. A few years ago we tried putting pictures of our kids and animals on our website in an attempt to promote our theme of "Families Helping Families." When we did a survey of our customers, however, we discovered that all they want is information. When you look at Tony's world-class website (www.tonyjeary.com), you will see his brand all over it, along with tons of information about making effective presentations.

Because people come to your site for information, it's important that they are able to get to that information quickly. Various studies have been conducted on how many clicks a visitor is willing to make to get to the information he is looking for. It seems that visitors are generally willing to click through three pages before giving up and going elsewhere to find what they are looking for. Just as the web makes it easy for people to find information, it also makes it easy for them to switch companies (or in your case, real estate agents) if they don't find what they're looking for. On the web, your competition is just one click away, so it's critical that you make your information as easily accessible as possible.

While your website can be as simple or as sophisticated as you want it to be, there are certain components you will want to include to make it an effective tool for your real estate customers. Keep in mind that interactive pages are very popular—pages that include forms the customer can fill out requesting some kind of action. On our website, sellers can fill out a form describing the home they want to sell, and we can email a free online marketing analysis of their home back to them. We also include forms for our buyers to fill out, giving the criteria for the type of home they want including the price range. Then we can send their data to our local Multiple Listing System (MLS) and get them set up in a Buyer Instant Notification (BIN) program that will email listings to them that match their criteria. This tool gives them the advantage of being among the first to see those listings. Our buyers can also get pre-qualified for a mortgage online. (Another advantage of these interactive forms is that they help you track your marketing dollars.)

If you include interactive forms on your website, it is crucial that you check your website several times a day, so you can respond in a timely manner. When we get a form from a buyer, we give the contact information to one of our buyer agents who immediately e-mails the buyer or makes a phone call if the telephone number is given. People often buy emotionally, and if you wait two or three days, you will likely miss the opportunity for a sale. Remember, too, that if they are filling out your form, they are likely filling out other real estate agents' forms as well. It's very important that you give them an immediate response.

We recommend these components for a real estate agents website—one that will provide a great working tool for your customers:

1. **Home Page/Welcome**—Give your guests reasons for exploring your website further and encourage them to contact you for their real estate needs.

2. **Your Company's Listings**—We include a link to our listings on every single page in our website. The more often your visitors see this link, the more likely they are to explore further. We use a rolling link that shows pictures of the homes, as well as the prices, and customers can click on the pictures for additional information on the homes.

3. **Testimonials**—Additionally, we include a testimonial on every page. Testimonials are powerful marketing tools.

4. **Home Search**—It's best to include several options for a home search. We suggest you include:
   a. Instant access to a public version of your local MLS to see all area listings. This service is available to real estate agents in most areas through an IDX provider (usually the larger real estate companies)
   b. Homes you are featuring
   c. Links to national listings databases (such as Homes.com, TheRealEstateBook.com, etc.), new home construction sites (like HomeBuilder.com), unique and luxury properties (such as LuxuryRealEstate.com or UniqueHomes.com), and international properties (such as Immobel.com)

5. **A Section for Buyers**—You want to list in this section all the reasons why buyers should select your real estate company to represent them. Then provide one or more options that

will lead them to the interactive form that will give you their contact information and a description of the home they want to buy. You may also want to appeal to first-time homebuyers by providing a page telling how you can help them. Then don't forget to include a page where buyers can get prequalified for a mortgage. *Each page in this section should have an interactive form for the customer to complete.*

6. **A Section for Sellers**—This section is a great place to convince sellers that your company is the best choice they could make for their real estate needs. You could include a page describing your in-home presentation, in which you give the sellers a free market analysis of their home, and then a page describing each special program you provide for sellers (such as a guaranteed home sale program or a quick cash-out sale program). It's a good idea to appeal to customers who are considering selling their homes themselves by providing facts that "For Sale by Owner" sellers need to know. *Be sure to include on each page a link to an interactive form for the sellers to complete, giving information about themselves and their home.*

7. **Local Information**—This link is a very popular section as well. Buyers especially want as much information as they can get about your town and the schools in your area.

8. **Resources**—This area is the place for you to feature any special offers you may make, links to your newsletter or national real estate newsletters, links to affiliates (roofers, mortgage companies, etc.), and special tools provided by your web-hosting company. (Ours provides market condition reports, a Java-based mortgage calculator, a real estate dictionary, etc.) Another great feature to include here is an "Ask Us Anything" form that allows the customer to e-mail

any questions they may have about real estate to you. This feature is another great way to capture a lead.

9. **Information About Your Company (About Us)**—Keep it short, but let them know your credentials. This section is also another great place for a link to your testimonial page. You can have a page here to list your guarantees as well, and a page for real estate agents only with a form they can use to send you referrals. Don't forget to include a contact page in this section that gives all of your contact information and allows the customer to e-mail you.

Keep in mind that your website needs to be clean, simple, and very user-friendly. If visitors have trouble navigating your site, they won't stay, and you will lose the lead. If they have to wade through a lot of text to find what they want, they won't stay either. Remember the three-click rule discussed earlier: It shouldn't take a visitor more than three clicks to get to the information they are looking for.

Some real estate companies provide a website to their agents for a very small monthly fee, and they even provide templates. They have links on their sites that lead customers to each agent's website. Customers who go to the Keller Williams site (www.KW.com) looking for our company for example can access our site from there. And since these larger companies are your source for the IDX listings (the public MLS listings for each area), you would be able to include that excellent tool on your site as well. If your company offers these services, it's a great way to build your website for less money.

We have found that for every 100 listings, it takes at least one full-time person and one part-time person to maintain your part of the website (your company branding, your listings, and anything else pertaining to your company) and keep it current. If you are a small company or an individual agent with only a few listings, you may be able to do it all yourself or with a part-time assistant. Again, *we can't emphasize enough how crucial it is to keep your information current and to respond to your leads in a timely manner.* Remember, your competitor is just a click away. If you don't keep the information current and respond promptly, it does little good to have a website in this age of technology where people have access to all of your competitors' websites and listings as well as yours.

A few weeks ago, Jim and I had a buyer who wanted to look at a $1.3 million home in our area. I called the agent and told her we had a buyer interested in looking at the property, and she told me to go to her website. I did that, and I e-mailed her that we wanted to see the property within the next three days because I was leaving on a business trip. Three weeks later we still hadn't heard from the real estate agent. I would imagine that she would have one upset seller if he knew that she had never responded to our request to show the house. We showed our buyer other homes of course, but the point is that the other real estate agent's apathy or lack of technology communication is limiting the showings on her homes. Why lose any business?

Obviously, if you want to have a website that generates 40 percent of your leads, it is not a tool to treat flippantly. We really believe that if you do not take your website seriously, you are making a grave mistake. You run the risk of actually alienating potential clients. We recommend that you build a powerful website that will allow you to compete in today's technology age, and advertise it on every venue available to you—your signs, your vehicles, your business cards, in the newspaper, on television, on your sold cards, and anywhere else you think people may see it. And, most importantly, make sure your web hosting company is getting you on the best search engines possible.

Important POINTS

1. Building your website to clearly reflect your brand will make it one of the most powerful tools in your marketing arsenal.

2. About 40 percent of our leads come from our website now, compared to 10 percent just three years ago.

3. It is much less expensive—and much more effective—to advertise homes on a website than it is to advertise them in the newspaper.

4. It is very important to plaster your web address on everything you do—newspaper advertising, television advertising, billboards, sold cards, business cards, etc. Your web address needs to appear everywhere people look—as a part of your brand—to drive people to your site.

5. For your website to be effective, you need to make sure you are listed with the best search engines to ensure that your name is among the top results when people are searching for a home in your area.

6. Your website should be consistent with all of your other marketing tools as far as colors, logo, pictures, slogan, etc.

7. Include interactive forms on your website for both buyers and sellers to complete, giving information about themselves and the homes they wish to buy or sell.

8. It is crucial to keep the information on your website current and to respond to your leads in a timely manner.

4

Presenting
One-on-One

**In Hawaii, Bob had run a very successful insur-
ance business.** But when he moved to Denton, Texas, late in
life, he decided to go into the real estate business. By the time we
met him he was 70 years old and had worked for two different real
estate companies in the Denton area. He was about ready to quit the
business. "I don't understand it," he told us. "I was very successful
in insurance, but I can't seem to break through in real estate."

"If you will go out every day and meet 20 people that you don't
know and tell them what you do for a living," Jim told him, "you will
have a phenomenal first year in the real estate business." Bob took
Jim's advice. He talked to people in the grocery store. He talked to

people when he walked in the mornings, and he even drove around neighborhoods looking for people to talk to. It worked! He built a $6 million business within his first year!

Presenting Your Business in One-on-One Encounters

As an agent, you have undoubtedly been told time and again that you need to talk to as many people as possible because real estate is a numbers game. But, like Bob, you may not know how to open a dialogue with people. *Mastering your presentation with just a couple of lines that will lead the conversation toward real estate will increase your numbers exponentially.*

Let's say you've gone to the convenience store, and the person behind the counter says, "It's really a pretty day outside." Your response to that should be something like, "Yes, it is. I'm in real estate, and these really pretty days are very valuable to me." Or you could say, "Yes, it is a beautiful day. I sell real estate, and we just can't have enough of these beautiful days." Similarly, if the person says, "It's really stormy outside," your response could be, "Yes, I'm a real estate agent, and these kinds of days make it hard to get out and show properties."

As a real estate company with an established office, we have the advantage of being able to bring people into our office. We currently have about eight people working in our office who are either past clients or acquaintances. The reason for that is that we often use the following line when we meet people that we like and respect: "You know, you would be great in my business." The usual answer is, "Oh, really? What business is that?" Our response, of course, is, "I'm in the real estate business." The funny thing is, they rarely ever say, "Oh, I've been dying to get into the real estate business." What they typically say is something like, "Oh, my sister needs to sell her house," or "My mom is looking for a house." This particular conversation opener was the one Bob used almost exclusively to build his business. It's very effective! Some of the people will actually end up joining your real estate team or doing business with you.

Once you use your lead-in line to direct the conversation toward real estate, it's easy to turn the dialogue toward talking about the person and finding out his or her real estate needs. *We always use a very low-key, low-pressure approach. You can't make people need to buy a house. They either do or they don't.* When you reach the point of Presentation Mastery with your scripts and dialogues, you will be able to very quickly qualify people to see if they do have a real estate need. You might say something very simple like, "I'm just curious. Are there any real estate needs that you might have right now that we can help you with?" Then, in a very non-threatening conversation, you can determine if you will be able to help them with their needs.

Ask people what you can do for them. Really, it's all about giving to someone before you ask to get something. It's okay with us if we are just a real estate resource for people for a while. Remember Tony's "principle of reciprocation" that we talked about in Chapter One—that people usually feel "beholden" to give something back when they receive something from you? At some point, the odds are that if you give you will get back. You can't lose by giving first, even if it's just information to help them lower their taxes.

You can use the lead-in lines we've discussed in any number of places: the grocery store, the gas station, the coffee shop, the cleaners, the mall, the doctor's office, your children's school and extracurricular activities, garage sales, the airplane, the library, the utility company, the post office, your church, the health spa—the possibilities are unlimited. You have to be ready with your presentation and be able to lead quickly into a conversation about your business. It really is a numbers game, and the more alert you are to keeping a business mentality when you meet people, the more your numbers will grow. You will need to talk to a lot of people to find just the few who need your services.

When an acquaintance initiates the conversation by asking, "What do you do for a living?" we normally say, "We are in the business of meeting and exceeding real estate expectations." But when we are the ones doing the approaching, we try to direct the conversation to meeting *their* real estate needs as quickly as possible. If you have a hard time knowing what to say, internalize these simple presentations and learn to present them very naturally when you meet people everywhere you go.

Most people love to talk about real estate. Try wearing a badge or a t-shirt with your company's name on it, and see how often people open the dialogue and start asking you questions about your company. If they see your shirt and they have a real estate need, they will open the conversation! When people do approach you, you want them to feel comfortable that their real estate needs will be met. We usually say something like: "I would be happy to meet and exceed your real estate expectations. Are you looking to buy a home or sell a home?" Then we ask them a few qualifying questions about their time frame and very quickly walk them through the process. "Bill, let me tell you how we can help you. The first thing we need to do is come out and look at your home to help you determine what the value is. Would a week day or a weekend be better?"

Remember, whether you are talking to people face-to-face or over the phone, you are not there to give them a sales presentation in that first encounter. You are simply focusing on getting an appointment. Sometimes real estate agents try to throw everything into that first conversation because they are afraid they won't get another chance. In reality, you are just building a relationship and a comfort level with that person; and once you find that there is a need, you want to set an appointment. Save your sales presentation for the set appointment. The last thing you want to do is to get into your presentation when the person is not in a place where he can sit down and sign a contract.

Remember, too, that time is one of your most precious commodities. Real estate agents who want to go to the highest level put a high premium on their time. It's easy to get so caught up in trying to get an appointment when you meet someone that you fail to qualify that person adequately. You don't want to waste your time or his if his motivation to buy or sell a home is not high enough. *We have learned to very quickly in the conversation slide in a great question to identify the person's level of motivation without making it seem like we are pushing the person for information.* Rather than risk assuming that they are more qualified than they really are, we simply ask something like this: "Just to make sure that my motivation matches your motivation and I'm not calling you all the time if you don't want me to, on a scale of one to ten, with 10 being you need to buy a house yesterday and one being you don't care if you buy a house all year, would you rate for me your motivation to buy a home from me please?"

When you look at your database, if you see mostly people who are a four, five, or six on the motivational scale, it would be better for you to go out and meet new people who are highly motivated, rather than trying to breathe life into the ones you have. They are the only ones who can change their motivation—you can't! You *can*, however, ask them what is missing to make them an eight, nine, or a ten, and you can help direct them over any hurdles they may have to get there, but you can't increase their motivation for them. Until that happens, you can be a real estate resource for them and "drip" on them on a regular basis to keep your name in front of them.

It's very important to convey confidence when you are talking to people, and the best way to do that is to internalize and practice until you reach Presentation Mastery™. Tony Jeary's IPRESENT model (see page 103) that he covers in detail in his books helps people understand the eight essential practices of successful presenters. Maybe it's time for you to evaluate your confidence and the way you come across. Everyone can use a tune up once in awhile in his or her presentation skills. Lack of confidence often comes across as groveling, which is very distasteful for most people. You actually want to come from a place of discovery—making sure you are a match for this person and they are a match for you. You want to be able to turn down business that may not be the right match, and if you are "tap dancing," it is difficult to bow out gracefully. The ideal situation is one in which the clients want the deal more than you do. They can usually sense any apprehension on your part, so it is important to internalize the scripts and dialogues to build your confidence and not be talking out of desperation.

Networking, whether it is with complete strangers, other agents, or a group of people with whom you meet regularly, is a huge part of your real estate career, and it helps you on both sides of the coin. One of the reasons your clients pay you a commission is your ability to network with other agents and buyers to get their homes sold. A lot of inter-agency networking goes on in real estate—agents checking with their peers to see what listings they have. The more homes you have on the market, the more other agents will want to network with you.

On the other side of the coin, if you are networking with a group of people you don't know to increase your business, you would use the same one-on-one scripts and dialogues we discussed above. But a great source of business for us is our networking group that we meet with every month—a group of business people who have agreed to refer clients to each other. If you decide to start a networking group like this, be sure to include only one business from each industry (one plumber, one decorator, one builder, etc.) For your monthly meetings, you can have one topic to discuss, have several people make presentations about their businesses, or just meet socially. We go around the room and allow each person to tell just a little about his or her business each month and who they've done business with from the group recently, so your presentations for this type of group will be more for a group setting than a one-on-one situation. For a small fee, we put ads for the people in our networking group in our presentation folder that we leave with all of our buyers and sellers, so they get a lot of exposure to people who are in the market for their services.

Presenting Your Business over the Phone

When people call you on the phone for their real estate needs, your scripts and dialogues will consist mostly of questions that will lead to an appointment to meet with the caller. Over the years, we have identified the exchange of information that most successfully leads to that end.

Presenting to Sellers over the Phone

When you are selling a home, your presentation actually begins before you ever go out to view the home and meet the sellers. When someone calls our office and says she wants to list her home with us, she is asked a series of questions. (See our Listing Qualifier Form on page 88.) Our staff person asks where she is moving, how soon does she need to be there, and whether she has talked to any real estate agents in that area. (Many real estate agents neglect the referral possibilities in building their businesses. Referral commissions are a great source of revenue.) Then she is asked what she owes on her

Listing Questionnaire

Today's Date: _____   Contact Name: _____

Address of property your wanting to Sell: _____

Names of all property Owners: _____

Their Address if Different _____

Phone Numbers: Home_____

Cell _____   Work _____

Email Address _____

Why are you selling your home? _____

May we assist you in finding another property? _____

How soon do you have to be there? _____

How long have you owned this property? _____

Do you know what you currently owe on the property? _____

Do you have a price in mind of what you think your
home should be listed for?_____

Have you had the property on the market for sale before? _____

If so why did you think it did not sell? _____

Are you considering FSBO? _____

How soon are you ready to List? _____

How did you hear about McKissack Group? _____

Brief Description of your Home:

Approximate Square Feet under Heat/Air _____

Age of home _____   # of bedrooms _____

# of baths _____   Garage_____

# of living areas_____ Fireplaces _____

Fence type _____   # of stories_____

Foundation type _____ Type of flooring _____

Any Outside Improvements such as Pool/Spa, Sprinkler,
Covered Patio, Storage Buildings, etc. _____

Have you made any other improvements?_____

Anything need to be replaced or repaired? _____

_____

What is convenient date/time to meet with all parties? _____

APPOINTMENT DATE:_____   APPOINTMENT TIME: _____

property, what she feels is the current value of her home, whether she is considering going FSBO (For Sale by Owner), and whether she will be interviewing another agent. Some agents are uncomfortable with those last two questions, but our thinking is that it is better to be prepared than to be caught off guard later on. Also, if someone is considering going FSBO, the presentation will change just a little. Then she is asked how soon she is planning to list her home, how she came about calling the McKissack Group, and when would be a good time for someone from our team to come out and put her home on the market.

Presenting to Buyers over the Phone

Typically when a buyer calls our office, they are calling about a property they saw in an ad. A good friend of ours has a great script called "Turning Ad Calls into Dollars," and she has graciously given her permission to include it in this book with just a few of our personal tweaks:

> OBJECTIVE: To set an appointment for you, the Buyer's Agent; an appointment for your [Listing] Agent if the caller owns a home, and to have them pre-qualified prior to showing homes.
>
> SETTLE FOR: Placing them on the BIN program and following up with phone calls.
>
> PROSPECT: Calling on an ad or sign.
>
> RESPONSE: I can help you with that, but first may I ask which magazine you are calling from? (Or: Where did you see the ad?) (If they are calling on a sign or if they mention the exact magazine, you do not need to ask, of course.)
>
> One other question: Are you working with an agent? I assume since you're calling me you're not working with another agent.
>
> YES: I'll fax this information immediately to your agent.

NO: Thank you. I'd be happy to help. I can schedule a time to look at some property, if you'd like. Would _____ or _____ be better?

Set Appointment:

IF NO POSITIVE RESPONSE: I can certainly understand. Here's one thing I can do to help you get started in a positive direction in looking for your dream home. We have a lender that will pre-qualify you for a loan. That way when you find the right home, the seller will have no hesitation accepting your offer because you are pre-qualified. We also offer a free credit report if you allow the lender to call you. That's a $65 value. Where might I have the lender call you in the next hour? (Then call or page your lender—whatever it takes to have them call the seller back within the next hour.)

IF NO RESPONSE: Another thing that we offer FREE TO YOU is to put you on our BIN program. By telling me what you are looking for and the area you are looking in, I can enter that information into our computer program that links directly into the Multiple Listing Service. Then every day I can pull the new listings that fit your needs and call, fax, or mail those listings to you. Or if you have e-mail, the system will e-mail you directly the listings that meet your criteria as they are entered into the MLS system. We have many people on this program now, and they love it. Would you like to take advantage of this FREE offer?

Buyer's Agency Contract:

There is one thing I want you to understand about this Buyer's Agency Contract, and that is that it is a benefit to you. After you sign this agreement and make me your agent, I can answer you in a paragraph instead of a sentence when it comes to the seller's motivation. Now in this contract, it states that you must purchase your home from me for the duration of the contract. Some agents want you to sign with them for six months to a year. I think that is ridiculous! If they drop the ball, then you still have to buy from them for that entire year. That doesn't make much sense, does it? My duration is whatever you feel comfortable with. One day? One week? One month? How long do you want the duration to be?

Asking for the Appointment:

Remember, you are always going for the appointment. Ask yourself this question: What questions could I ask that are harder for them to say no to?

WHEN could we get together?

HOW SOON could I show you the home?

IS THERE A BEST TIME to show you the property?

COULD I SHOW YOU THE PROPERTY THIS AFTERNOON? Or would this evening be better?

Qualifying Questions:

These questions are not necessarily in the order in which you will use them.

- Do you live in the area? (If not . . .) Is this your first visit to (your city)?
- Where are you from?
- How long have you been looking for a home?
- Where do you live now?
- How long have you lived there?
- Do you own your home or are you renting?
- Will it be necessary to sell your home before you buy one (or finish your lease period)?
- Approximately how much do you feel you will realize from the sale of your home?
- How many are in your family? Oh, then you have _____ children? What are their ages?
- Have you seen any homes you like yet?
- If so, what prevented you from buying them?
- How soon had you thought about making a move when we find the right home?
- How long will you have today to see homes?
- How long have you been seriously looking for a home?
- Where are you employed?

- How long have you been employed there?
- What is your position?
- How would you describe the home you would like to buy today?
- Would you describe your present home for me? What do you like best?
- If we find the right home today, would you be in a position to proceed?

Buyer Specialist:

What kind of agent would you like to have represent you? One who works with buyers, sellers, mortgage companies, title companies, and handles all the paperwork and everything else in between? Or would you rather work with an agent whose sole job description is to help you find the perfect home? You see, I'm a Buyer's Specialist, and that's what I do. I only work with homebuyers, so I'm able to preview over 200 homes per month, and I know the market better than anyone. So tell me, which type of agent would you rather work with?

Wanna Buy It?

The way that I'll know you are interested in purchasing one of the homes that I'll show you is that I will simply ask you if you would like to buy it. Would that be okay with you? And by the way, if I forget to ask, will you remind me?

There are several things included in the script above that we want to emphasize. We can't stress enough how powerful a tool the BIN (Buyer Instant Notification) program is. A buyer's biggest fear is that he will not be able to find out quickly enough about the best properties. In our initial contact with a buyer we simply ask, "Have you ever driven by a great home for sale and called on it, just to have the people say it is already under contract? One of the ways we can keep that from happening to you is to put you on what we call our BIN program. This program notifies you by e-mail or by phone whichever you prefer when a property comes available that matches your criteria." We ask about BIN even before we meet with them face-to-face because it ensures that we will get the buyer's name and phone number.

Another very important thing to remember is to make sure that the buyer is not working with any other real estate agents. The way we handle that situation is to simply ask: "I assume since you are calling me that you are not working with any other real estate agents. Is that correct?" You don't want to waste your time if they are under a Buyer Representative Agreement with someone else. If they are interviewing other real estate agents we have a list of 21 questions that we suggest they ask to help them find the agent that will work best for them.

21 Questions Form

If you are interviewing other REALTORS® ask them these important 21 questions. You should assume the agent is full-time, and is a member in good standing of The National Association of Realtors.

1. How long have you been selling real estate?
   The McKissack Group has been selling in Denton County since 1982.

2. How many homes do you sell a year?
   The McKissack Group averages 300 annually vs. 15 by the average agent.

3. How many homes have you sold in your career?
   The McKissack Group has represented over 2500 families and has been #1 in Denton County for the past 13 years!

4. What is your average time on the market versus the Multiple Listing Service (MLS)?
   McKissack properties sell on average 45 days faster!

5. What is your average list to sell ratio, and how does that compare to the rest of the MLS?
   McKissack properties bring on average 1.5% higher sales price to list price. That is $1500.00 more money in your pocket on a $100,000.00 sale! This means less showing headaches for you!

6. Where do you rank in your office? Top Lister? Top Seller? For how many years?
   The McKissack Group has consistently been #1 in Denton County for the past 9 years!

7. Where do you rank in your company, franchise. . .locally, internationally? How many years?
   The McKissack Group ranks from #1 to #3 in various national rankings.

8. Where does your individual office rank in the MLS? For how many years?
   The McKissack Group has ranked #1 for the past several years!

9. How strong is your name recognition in the market place?
   The McKissack Group receives numerous calls from name recognition alone!

10. If I buy one of your listings, will you buy my home?
    If a buyer needs to sell their home first, before buying my home, will you buy their home?
    The McKissack Group offers a Guarantee Sale Program.

11. What percentage of your accepted contracts close? What percentage fall apart?
    Having a team of professionals provides a much higher percentage of closings meaning less inconvenience to you.

12. What is your marketing plan?
    The McKissack Group advertises in magazines, newspaper, brochures, 24-hour talking ad and the #1 Web-site in the area.
    * Where and how often will you advertise our home?
      The McKissack Group will advertise in as many places and as often as necessary according to the market.
    * Would you provide us with professional four-color brochures of our home?
      The McKissack Group provides inside & outside brochures!
    * Will you provide Internet advertising?
      Yes! We take multiple photos & provide Virtual Tour if necessary!

13. What lead generation system(s) do you have to develop an inventory of buyers for your listings? Where are they? Who manages them?
    The McKissack Group offers a cross reference computer system to match literally hundreds of buyers with your property!

14. How many qualified buyers are you currently working with? Is there a follow up system?
    The McKissack Group maintains 50+ buyers on average with their marketing plan giving you a better opportunity for multiple offers.

15. How many full-time assistants do you have?
    Do you have a listing coordinator, a closing coordinator, a team coordinator?
    The McKissack Group provides a staff of highly trained assistants to monitor your property!

16. Do you have enough buyer leads to require a buyer showing agent or agents?
    The McKissack Group has a staff of full time Buyer Consultants available to handle all buyer leads.

17. Do you provide us with written activity reports of the showings and prospective buyer & REALTOR® comments?
    The McKissack Group provides feedback through email, mail & phone calls!

18. Do you have a mission statement?
    The McKissack Group has had one for several years!

19. Will you give us your professional opinion on how to prepare our home for showings?
    The McKissack Group is always honest. We will tell you what you NEED to hear!

20. Do you have a list of references that we may call?
    The McKissack Group has many including 1000's of past surveys.

21. Do you have a Moving Van?
    The McKissack Group is so confident they will sell your home, they purchased a Moving Van in order to assist you!

We mentioned in the first part of this chapter how important it is to qualify the buyer by identifying where he is on the motivation scale. "Mr. Smith, I will not call you every day if you don't want me to. Just to make sure that my motivation matches your motivation, on a scale of one to 10, with 10 being you need to buy a house yesterday and one being you don't care if you buy a house all year, would you rate for me your motivation to buy a home from me please?" You don't want to waste your time or the buyer's if your motivations don't match.

You may also find helpful the Buyer Questionnaire Form we use when a buyer calls our office.

Buyer Questionnaire Form

Buyer Consultant _____

Date _____

Clients Name _____

Email _____

Address _____

_____

Phone 1 _____ Phone 2 _____

Fax_____ Cell _____

How did you hear about the McKissack group?

_____

_____

Have you had an opportunity to talk with a lender?

_____

_____

How long have you been looking? _____

Are you working with another agent? _____

Who? _____

Have you made a commitment to work with that agent? _____

If I gave you 100% of our time, will you be willing to work exclusively with the McKissack Group _____

If not, why? _____

How soon do you need to move? _____

Do you own or rent? _____

Must you sell/complete a lease before buying? _____

What do you want your monthly payment to be? _____

Areas you are interested in? _____

How many are in your family? _____

Notes/Special Requirements? (i.e.3/2/2 etc.) _____

_____

_____

P O I N T S

1. Mastering your presentation with just a couple of lines that will lead the conversation toward real estate will increase your numbers exponentially.

2. Use a very low-key, low-pressure approach. You can't make people need to buy a house. They either do or they don't.

3. When you reach the point of Presentation Mastery™ with your scripts and dialogues, you will be able to quickly qualify people to see if they do have a real estate need.

4. Remember whether you are talking to people face-to-face or over the phone you are not there to give them a sales presentation in that first encounter. You are simply trying to get an appointment.

5. Ask a great question that identifies the person's level of motivation.

6. It's very important to convey confidence when you are talking to people, and the best way to do that is to internalize and practice until you reach Presentation Mastery™.

TWO

Servicing Your Clients Through Presentation Mastery

5

Presenting
For the Sale

Securing a Listing, Working with a Buyer, or Negotiating an Offer

We were fairly new in the business, had never heard of the consultative presentation, had very few systems in place, and were more or less shooting from our hip pockets with trial-and-error tactics. We had received a call from a gentleman, but there was some confusion as to what he even wanted from us. Jim's brother, Brad, and I went on the appointment to—hopefully—secure the listing. Rather than assuming what we *thought* he wanted, Brad and I decided we would just ask, up front. "On a scale of one to ten, with ten being a great meeting and one being a total waste of your time, what one thing has to happen tonight so that you will feel that this is a great meeting?" we asked. He was an engineer (a very high "C" in the DISC Profiler), and he was silent for what seemed like forever. Then he finally said, "Well, I have actually already chosen the McKissack Group to list my property. I guess the main thing is for us to decide what price we need to list my house for, so I can be out within the next 90 days." Had we not asked that question, we would have spent the next 25 or 30 minutes telling him how wonderful the McKissack Group was and trying to sell him on listing with our company. It would have been a total waste of both his time and ours!

If you are going to be in the business of meeting and exceeding your clients' expectations, you have to find out what those expectations are. You have to move to a consultative approach to find out what is most important for them in a transaction. Most of the time when there is a problem, it is because of a miscommunication about what was expected. We have found that the best way to find out what is expected is to just ask.

There is a difference between a *functionary* real estate agent and a *fiduciary* real estate agent. A functionary agent tells the client what to do or tells them what they think they want to hear, while a fiduciary agent finds out what his client's needs really are. A functionary agent assumes what the client's needs and expectations are and sets out trying to meet and exceed expectations that they don't even know about! The fiduciary agent rises to the highest level by asking great questions and assuming nothing.

The Consultative Presentation to Sellers

A great listing presentation starts with asking great questions. *Before* you go out, make sure you are prepared for the presentation. In our office, immediately after the initial contact, we send out what we call a "pre-sale package" that includes information about our team—who we are and how our team works. We have found that sending this package out helps keep our "sell and tell" to a minimum during the presentation.

When you get to the home, it's very important to begin building rapport with the sellers right away. (Ask if you can sit at the kitchen table or at the dining room table, if they prefer, or stand at a kitchen counter; but the last place you want to make your presentation is in the living room where it is less conducive to taking care of business.) Then, while you are looking at their home, build rapport with them. We have found that using the acronym FORD—Family, Occupation, Recreation, and Dreams—helps us steer the conversation toward finding out as much as we can about them and their real estate needs.

Tony Jeary offers eight essential practices of successful presenters (IPRESENT) to help people hone their sales and presentation skills, and this is a great place to put those strategies into practice.

IPRESENT

I	Involve your audience
P	Prepare your audience
R	Research your presentation arsenal
E	Explain the 'why'
S	State Management
E	Eliminate the unknowns
N	kNow your audience
T	Tailor your message

As you are going through their home and noticing various items, ask questions about their family, what they do for a living, how they spend their spare time, and what they hope to do in the future. Use all four categories to help you build rapport. A trophy in their son's room, for example, might elicit a statement like: "Tell me about your family. It looks like you have a great little soccer player here." Or you can ask questions like: "What do you do for fun?" "If you had a dream home where would it be?" You are not only gathering information to help you find the perfect home for them, but you are building a relationship with them as well.

We have found that there are generally two kinds of real estate agents when it comes to building rapport: One who needs to be reminded to do it, and one who needs to be reminded when it is time to *stop* doing it. Remember, your time is valuable and so is your clients'! Know when it is time to get down to the business at hand.

When you go back to the kitchen table to talk about the listing, stay in the consultative presentation mode. We have found that everyone who goes into a meeting or a class or a seminar has some expectation of what they think that meeting will be about, and that expectation is either going to be fulfilled or they will come out disappointed. So, as we discovered with the engineer, your first question should be something like: "What is your expectation of our meeting tonight? What one thing needs to happen to make this a great meeting?"

There is one statement that most real estate agents dread to hear: "Tell me why I should list my home with you." The worst thing you want to do is to start groveling or tap dancing to give them an answer, and then start "telling and selling." We have a *great* response to that question: "Actually, Mr. and Mrs. Seller, one of three things is going to happen here this evening. Number one, you may choose the McKissack Group to sell your home, and that would be great. Number two, you may not choose the McKissack Group, and that would not be so great. Number three, we may not be able to take your listing." At that point, you will probably get either a blank stare or the question, "Why would you not be able to take my listing?"

Even if they don't ask, you still need to explain. "I know that may sound strange to you, so let me explain. You may have a need or an expectation in the sale of this home that we don't feel like we can meet or exceed. If we come to that point, we would rather let you down now than disappoint you later. Is that fair enough?" *You want to leave yourself an out, and you want to let the sellers know that you don't take every listing.* If they have expectations that are unrealistic (like wanting $200,000 for a home that will only sell for $150,000), you don't want to take the listing and spend your money, time, and effort to market that property. You will only wind up disappointing them, and you don't want to allow that to happen.

Even if the sellers don't ask "the question," you still want to tell them the three things that might happen at the meeting because you want to *control the dynamics of the presentation.* You could say something like, "Let's switch gears here for a minute, and let's talk about what might actually happen in our meeting this evening." Then you go into the same dialogue: "One of three things will happen here today. . . ." People tend to want to choose their real estate agent based on the price they determine for their home rather than choosing the one who has the best strategy for getting their home sold. What you are doing by explaining the three options that could happen is moving them from emotion to logic.

Then you will want to transition into a discussion about their needs by saying something like: "Let's talk about what your needs and expectations are in the sale of your home. On a scale of one to 10, with 10 being this is a great transaction—it exceeds all of your expectations and you go and tell all of your friends they need to use the McKissack Group to sell their home—what one thing do we need to accomplish in this transaction for that to happen?" You are looking for what's most important for them in that sale. They are usually going to say one of two things: time or price. If they say, "I want a good price," you want to say, "Define good price for me."

Remember, any room you leave for assumption is room for error. You need to be very clear about what they mean. If they say to you, "I want to get $50,000 in equity," you want to dig deeper and ask, "Why is it important for you to get $50,000 in equity?"

Then you ask, "If we could make the transaction a 10-plus, what would it be?" Again, they will usually say time or price—whichever they didn't mention first. If they say something like, "To get my home sold quickly," you will want to ask them to define "quickly." If they say, "I want to sell my home in 90 days," you want to ask, "Why is it important to get your home sold in 90 days?" You are digging deeper to find out where the emotion is coming from because when they get an offer you may have to remind them what was important to them.

We suggest that you take it even one step farther and ask, "If we could make it a ten-plus-plus, what would it be?" You want to get their top three needs. This last one is a little bit harder to extract, but they normally say it is communication. **Statistics from NAR tell us that the number one complaint from selling consumers is that there was not adequate communication with their real estate professionals in the sale of their homes.** So they will typically say something like: "I want you to communicate with me on a regular basis." Again, you want to ask them to define "regular basis" because your regular basis may be different than theirs. But also be sure to ask *how* they would prefer that you communicate with them—by phone or by email.

Then you want to clarify the priority of their top three needs to make sure you are on the same page with the sellers. You might say something like this: "If we got your home sold at top dollar, but we didn't get it sold in 60 days, would that be okay?" What you might discover is that even though they mentioned money first, the time factor is actually the most important thing for them. You need to know which is most important because that is how you are going to meet and exceed their expectations.

After you determine your sellers' three most important needs, you design your presentation to address those needs, whatever they are. Remember though that no matter what their three top needs may be, it is very important to include the statement about the three things that could happen at the meeting. If you don't, it could be very awkward trying to get out of taking the listing if the situation warrants it.

Pricing is usually in the top two needs that sellers will list. When you move into the part of your presentation that addresses pricing, you need to communicate to your sellers that choosing a real estate agent based on the price they determine for their home is the worst thing they can do. A great agent will tell their clients what they need to hear rather than what they want to hear. One of the ways we move people away from that stance is to give them information. People will normally act on what they self-discover rather than on what we tell them. As a rule, none of the myriad reasons *we* give them for pricing their home correctly will do any good. So the first thing we do is show them current information on homes that have recently sold, homes that have been rejected (the expired MLS listings), and homes that will be their competition (those currently on the market that will either cause our buyers' home to sell or will sell because of our buyers' home). Then, rather than lecturing or telling them what to do, we get them into an experiential mode of self-discovery. We either put them in the car and take them to see the competition, or we tell them a story about a client who did not price his home correctly, or we ask them a question: "If you were a buyer in today's market, based on the data we have just given you, what would you be willing to pay for this house?" We also give our clients the pricing graph and pyramid below that show two things: the longer a property is on the market the lower the price it brings, and the higher you go above market price for your home the smaller percentage of buyers you have. By giving them information that will help them self-discover, we help them make great decisions.

The Importance of Intelligent Pricing

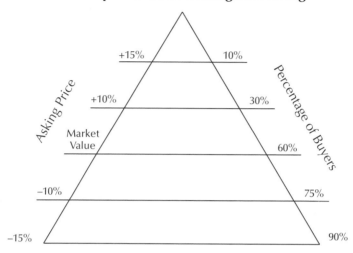

Selling Price vs. Timing

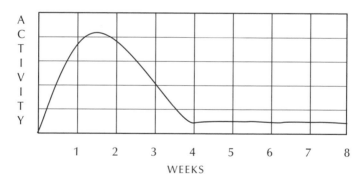

After we determine a price for their home, we show them how the market will either accept or reject the price. On a sheet of paper, we show the market on one side and the sellers and us on the other. *We want them to see the market as something we have to strategize together to beat—not something we are teaming up with against them.* Then we say to them, "We have either hit the mark on the pricing or we have missed it. The market will talk to us, and our job is to listen to what the market has to say, interpret it, and make very quick decisions to recommend that you make adjustments if we have missed it. NAR statistics tell us that no more than eight to 10 buyers should go through your home before you have an offer, so we will watch for those eight to 10 showings." We have to know their market well enough to know how long it will take to get those eight to ten showings, and we say to them, "In our current (buyers' or sellers') market, that should take no longer than _____ weeks." (In a buyers' market, it will take longer; in a seller's market, it will happen faster.) Then we say, "Here are the things that can happen: One, you have eight buyers look at your home, someone makes you an offer, and we're all happy. Two, we have eight showings, no one makes you an offer, and we're not so happy. The third thing that may happen is that we don't get eight showings. We feel better if we have eight showings and no offer, but the reality is that we are in no better position. Either way, it's the market's way of talking to us, and at that point we may have to look at making an adjustment." That conversation simply prepares the seller in the event you have to go back to them to recommend adjusting their price, and they know what to expect.

We also tell our clients, "The market is always moving. The only difference between the market for homes and the stock market is a little bit of emotion. If you were selling stock today, there would be a price per share that you could get for it. You don't get to say, 'I want $5 more or $10 more.' Whatever the price is for that day, that's the price you have to sell it for. Real estate is exactly the same way, except for a little bit of range for emotion. The buyer may be willing to pay just a little bit more, so we have to come up with a range and determine if we have missed the market or we are on it."

We have found that this discussion about how the market speaks to us is a very important part of the presentation that we don't ever want to skip. There is nothing more awkward than for you to have a great rapport with your sellers and then have the market not respond the way you thought it should after you list their home. When that happens, they usually end up disappointed in you, and you feel intimated. However, if you make it a point to show your sellers that you are working with them as a team to beat the market, you are always prepared for what may happen.

This presentation has been phenomenally successfully for us because it gets down to the core of what our clients' needs are rather than selling and telling all about us. It also puts us at a very high level of integrity with our clients. It's very helpful for new agents because the focus is not on what they have (or haven't) done, but on what the clients' needs are. The only "show and tell" we do is to tell the clients how we market homes. If it's a sellers' market, however, we very seldom even have to bring it up because the homes are selling so quickly. If it is a buyers' market, the sellers are usually very adamant about wanting to know how we are going to market their home. We have to show them, based on the current market, that our marketing tactics are working.

You may remember that we use the IVR system, an 800-number call-in system that tracks what marketing sources the calls are coming from. With this system, we are able to show our sellers our marketing sources that are receiving the best response. We would also be able to show them examples of where the market is rejecting the price, the location, or something else about the property—when the calls are coming in from the marketing sources, but the home is not selling. This system gives excellent data to help you strategize with the sellers to determine the best path for them.

It is during this part of the presentation that we ask the clients to pull out the pre-sale package we mailed to them, and we go through *very quickly* and tell about our team, how we work, and how we are able to sell over 350 homes a year. We have some sample marketing pieces in there, and we tell them what our strategy will be for marketing their home. This aspect, intentionally, is a very small piece of our selling presentation. Remember, we want to focus on the clients and their needs, not on us and our company. We like to keep the presentation 90 percent consultative and 10 percent sell and tell.

The last part of our presentation is handling objections. When you are handling objections, you want to remember several things:

1. Never debate.
2. Listen carefully. We tend to hear half of what our clients are saying, and then assume the rest. If you are not sure, ask for clarification. Always break something down to the simplest form before you respond.
3. Stay out of judgment and into curiosity.
4. Persist and stay calm.
5. Keep the clients in logic rather than emotion.
6. Don't be attached to the outcome.

Dealing with objections is where many agents resort to groveling and "selling and telling." In actuality, you need to have three scripts ready for any objection. You need to practice them daily and know them by heart before you ever get to the presentation, so that the minute someone gives you that objection the answer rolls off your tongue naturally.

The first objection you will probably receive is commission. Someone may ask, "Would you lower your commission?" The response I like best to this objection is, "My policy on reducing my commission is this," and then you tell them what your policy is. People understand policy. (By the way, our policy on reducing commission is this: One, if the clients bought their house in the past six months and are selling it at a loss, we will reduce our commission. Two, if they are buying another home from us and are buying up, we reduce our commission.) Some people will be adamant and push a little bit more, but at least one of your responses should satisfy them. Another response could be a question: "I'm just curious. Is it really the amount of commission you pay that's important, or the money you net? If I am able to negotiate a buyer up higher and make more money for you, does it really matter to you what I make for doing that?" Or your response could be, "Have you found someone else who is willing to reduce their commission, and that's why you are asking?" If they say yes, I often come back with something like, "If someone is that willing to give away their own money, how willing will they be to give away yours?" If the client is still adamant, you will have to make a decision. Another response I like is, "No, that would be a win/lose relationship, and I like win/win or there is no deal. If I did it for you, I would have to do it for everyone else."

Another objection you may get is that another real estate agent has promised to get them more money for their home. A great response for this objection is this: "Let me share with you how that would be a lose for you and a win for that agent. If they put that price out to the marketplace, they are going to get calls immediately. Would you agree? Those buyers are going to realize that your home is priced above market, but that real estate agent is going to be able to take those buyers and sell them another home. So it's a win for them and a lose for you because you still do not have your needs met." But again, you may get to the point with this objection that you have to make a decision. When someone is adamant about listing their home too high, we only agree to take it if their motivation is high enough. If it is, they will get realistic about the price because they have to sell. If they are not motivated, this would be the place you would say, "Remember I told you the three things that could happen this evening, and the third one was that you may have a need or an expectation that I don't feel that I can meet or exceed? I think we might have just reached that point. So what I would like to do is refer you to someone who specializes in properties listed above market price. If that doesn't work out, we would love to discuss helping you in the future."

The only other objection we normally get is that the sellers might want to list their home for a shorter length of time than we have on the listing agreement. This one is easy for us. We just tell them that we have an "easy exit" clause in our agreement that says that if at any point they are not happy with our services, they just need to let us know, and we will release them from the listing.

If you have done your presentation properly, the closing is easy and can actually happen rather quickly. In fact, we basically ask for the close throughout our presentation, gearing it toward our clients' needs. When we are talking about marketing, for example, we might say, "Do you see how this type of marketing could get your home sold in 60 days (or get you that top dollar that you are looking for on your home)?" Or, "Can you see how listing your home with us could get you moved to California in the time frame you want?" By getting affirmative remarks throughout the presentation, we simply say at the conclusion something like, "Based on what we have talked about this evening, I feel like we have the makings of a great relationship. Would you like to go ahead and get your home on the market this evening?" Often they say yes and start completing the paperwork.

If their response to that question is no, however, we ask, "What would prevent you from putting your home on the market?" They may say something like, "I have four more real estate agents I want to talk to." Our response to that would be, "That's great! After you talk to those four agents, if you feel that we are the ones that might meet and exceed your expectations, would you list your home with us then?" If they say yes, we might ask,

"Let me ask you are you meeting with those other real estate agents because you feel obligated since you have set the appointment? Or are you meeting with them because you still feel like they might have something better to offer?"

If they are just meeting with them out of obligation, I might say, "Well I have to tell you, one of the most important assets we all have is time, and unfortunately we can't make more of it. I know if it were me and you were already going to list your home with someone else, I would rather you let me know, so I can either spend time with my family or move on to someone else. If you would like, I will cancel those appointments for you." If it's really something they want to do, we give them a list of questions to ask the other real estate agents.

When we ask if there is anything that would prevent them from putting their home on the market, they may also say something like, "I'm just really not sure about this price." Our response to that would be, "Other than price, is there anything else that would keep you from putting your home on the market?" After we get all the objections out on the table, we go back and talk about each one.

The main thing is that you need to feel comfortable enough to ask the hard questions. Occasionally people have their own agendas, and you don't want to do business with someone who doesn't want to do business with you. It's much better to find that out up front than two weeks down the line after you have put time, effort, and money into marketing their home. You want them to feel okay if they don't believe you are a match for them. If you have given them enough opportunities for an "out" throughout your presentation, both of you will feel comfortable if that ends up being the case.

From time to time a seller will say—after our presentation—that he would love to list his home with us, but he has a relative or friend who is a real estate agent and feels obligated to list with that person. Our response to that is usually something like this: "Let me ask you a question. If you knew there was an agent out there who would get you more money for your home in a shorter amount of time with the least amount of hassle, would you still list your house with your (mother, brother, sister . . .)?" Most of the time, people just don't stop to think about what they are losing and may change their minds if you help them look at the situation realistically.

After we get the listing, we leave "homework" for our sellers to do: We give them a Seller's Disclosure Form to complete, as well as another form that we call our "If" Form. Basically, this form asks them to list important features of the home that they would want potential buyers to know. This form helps us write the ad for the home, and it tells us what the seller thinks is important about the home. Then the next day, we have an assistant go out and measure the home and pick up their homework (We ask the sellers to leave it on the kitchen table.). Then she comes back and enters all the information into MLS, and we put the sign in their yard, put the lock box on their door, and get them on the market that day. Then our assistant loads information about the home onto our website.

Communication with the sellers after you get the listing is critically important. We believe it is important to communicate with your sellers after every showing. In our office, we have one person who tracks all the showings on all of our listings. They call the agents who have shown the homes and get feedback on every showing, and then we communicate that to our sellers. It has taken us years to get to this point, but we have decided to benchmark and trend communication with our clients. We started out by making a verbal commitment to our clients while we were making the presentation that we would communicate every two weeks. Then, because we under promise and over deliver, we would communicate every seven to 10 days instead. We are now in a buyer's market in our area, and communication with our sellers is even more important. So we communicate with our sellers every week as well as after every showing until we get an offer on the property. Sometimes we have to tell them that the agent didn't respond, but we tell them that's the way the market speaks to us. If the buyers were interested in their home, their agent would be tracking us down.

The Consultative Presentation to Buyers

When we receive a call from buyers, our main goal is to get them into our office and do a consultative presentation with them to assess their needs.

When our buyers' agents talk to buyers on the phone, the first thing they ask is whether they are working with a real estate agent. If they say yes, they tell them that they will be glad to get with their agent to arrange for them to look at the property. If they say no, they ask if they are first-time home buyers because usually first-time home buyers are less knowledgeable about the process of buying a home, which lets the agents know how to tailor their presentation.

Again, the objective is to get the buyer to come into the office, let them meet our buyers' agent, find out what their needs are, explain buyer representation to them, and get them comfortable with the concept. *We have found that when they come into our office, our chances of closing the buyer are much better than if we meet them at a property location.* It takes a face-to-face meeting to build a relationship of trust. Our agents are willing to go to the property if necessary when someone calls in on an ad or a sign, but with the goal of bringing them into the office. One thing our agents tell them that usually accomplishes that goal is that they will do what few other agents will do—put them in front of the multiple listing computer and custom design a search just for them, which will pull up all the properties in any given area that exactly meet their needs. Then they say, "If you can come here to our office and spend 30 minutes with me, I can save you hours of driving around and wasting your own gas. We can explain the whole process to you and get you started on the right track. How does that sound to you?"

When the clients come to the office, our agents give them a tour of the office and then sit down with them for a consultative presentation. The first thing they do is tell them the same thing the listing agents tell their sellers: "Mr. Buyer, there are three things that could happen in our meeting today. One, you could choose to work with me, and that would be great. Two, you could choose not to work with me, and that would not be so great. And three, I could choose not to work with you if you have needs and expectations that I don't feel I could meet. Does that sound fair?" Again, that's a very important part of the script because it gives you an out if the buyers' expectations are unrealistic.

The next thing they do is ask the buyers to complete a checklist telling how they heard about the McKissack Realty Group and how quickly they need to buy a home. Then they assess the buyers' level of motivation by using the program "Are You an A, B, or C Buyer?" *This is a very important step, because it lets you know how much time you should spend with the buyer at his current level of motivation.*

Are You an A, B, or C Buyer?

At the McKissack Realty Group, we want our motivation to match your motivation. This means that if you need to buy a home today . . . you probably want me to call you every time a new listing becomes available. Now if you are not really in a hurry to buy . . . you probably don't want me to call you every time a new listing becomes available (perhaps the mail would work better for you in this situation) Never the less, by completing this form you will help us make sure that we can match your motivation.

When touring McKissack Realty Group it doesn't take long to see how busy the Buyer department is. For you, the Buyer . . . that's a good thing. You want a Buyer Specialist who is active and really knows the market. Touring our office you probably also noticed our Buyer Activity Boards. These boards serve a couple of purposes. One is to enable us to match properties with specific Buyer needs. The second reason and the most important is to classify all of our Buyers by motivation. In order for our team to focus on your real estate needs we must first determine your motivation or your "readiness" to buy. Since all Buyers don't have the same needs . . . we categorize our Buyers by motivation as follows:

"A" Buyer   Our highest priority Buyer. These are people who have to buy a home now. They have either sold their existing home, transferred into town, or their lease has expired. In many cases they could potentially be homeless.

"B" Buyer   Our second highest priority Buyer. These are people who are ready to buy, except they have a home to sell first, have a lease to fulfill, or are in the stages of getting pre-approved.

"C" Buyer   Our third highest priority Buyer. These people may buy a home when the right one comes along. (low motivation)

As you can see . . . if you are a "B" or "C" Buyer doesn't mean you are less important to us. Your needs are paramount. It only means we are trying to find homes for the "A" Buyer's first. Remember you could quickly become an "A" Buyer and become top priority! We will always do our best to accommodate you. Should your motivation change at any time please let us know so we may adjust our motivation to match yours.

I/We've read the above and feel that I/We are a/an _____ Buyer(s)

Then our agents give the buyers an Agency Disclosure, a required piece of reading (in most states) for every prospective client, explaining who represents who in the transaction. A natural lead-in from that document is to go into an explanation of buyer representation. Our agents usually say something like, "When you call an agent from an ad or a yard sign, you will normally be talking to a listing agent who is representing the seller. You don't want that, do you? The best thing you can do for yourself, Mr. Buyer, is to have someone representing your interests as a buyer. In (some states), one agent cannot represent both parties. So the only way you can be represented by an agent who will fulfill the fiduciary obligations to you legally as we negotiate the terms for you is to sign what is called a Buyer Representation Agreement. There is no cost to you, but it gives you the assurance that the agent will be working solely in your best interest, not the sellers'. In a lawsuit, you wouldn't go ask the prosecuting attorney to defend you, would you? (Or, if a couple were getting a divorce, the wife would be a little apprehensive if the husband said, 'You need to use my attorney, and it will make this a lot easier,' wouldn't she?) Whether you choose me or anyone else, the best thing you can do for yourself is to get someone to represent you. There is no obligation to you, but should you decide to work with me, I want you to be totally comfortable with me. I have been doing this for ___ years and am pretty good at what I do."

Some buyers are hesitant to sign the Buyers' Representation Agreement, but the main thing they need to know is the difference between having representation and not having representation. We assure the clients that the agreement works for both them and the agent. Both parties sign the agreement. It assures the clients that the agent is committed to them and that they will get the benefit of having someone working very hard to find them the best deal possible in the shortest amount of time. It protects the agent by assuring that she will be paid for the time she invests in working with the clients. Most clients understand the concept of not wanting to work for free.

Buyers often don't understand how the process works, so we also explain to them that:

- If they are considering a new construction home, there is no price advantage for them to purchase the home from the builder without buyer representation. Our buyer specialists are in and out of new homes a lot, and they know which ones the builders want to get rid of quickly and which ones they are offering incentives on.
- We can represent them on a FSBO transaction.
- They benefit by having representation on the FSBO transactions because they have someone who is looking out for their needs (and making sure they don't pay too much for the property)
- As their buyer representative, we can answer their questions on pricing issues in much greater detail.

Our agents determine the duration of the Buyer Representation Agreement by the motivation level of the buyer. If the buyer needs to buy a home within two weeks, there is no reason to make the term of the agreement more than two weeks. If they are just beginning to look and are not highly motivated, a six-month term is usually preferred.

For many real estate agents, getting the Buyer Representation Agreement signed is a huge hurdle they would rather avoid. But to show you the impact it can make on your business, our closing ratios between the people who sign and those who don't is 3:1. And if we start with a fully qualified buyer whose expectations on buying a home are realistic, our closing ratio is 100 percent! Although there is controversy about whether the agreements are enforceable, real estate attorneys have advised us that they are just as enforceable as a listing agreement, and agents can file for lost commissions *and attorney fees* in a court of law. Just remember when completing the agreement to be specific about the area the agreement covers. (Our agents usually show our county, but some agents only show the city and/or the school district.) The more vague you are, the less enforceable the agreement is.

Although our buyers' agents gauge their timing and wording by the personality of the buyer (using their knowledge of the DISC Profiler), they are not hesitant to ask for the agreement. If the buyer is reluctant, they say something like: "I really want to work with you if you want to work with me, but I do need this agreement signed."

Once the buyers sign the agreement, it is usually a giant mental commitment for them. That commitment gives you the opportunity to earn their business and gain lifetime clients. We want to stress here how important it is to work hard to meet and exceed your clients' expectations after they sign the agreement. You are obligated and committed to those clients just as much as they are obligated to you.

The final objective in our presentation to buyers is to educate them on the current market. They may have heard that it is either a sellers' market or a buyers' market, and they may not be sure what that means. We educate them on the difference and then tell them that no matter what market we are in, the good houses go the fastest. They may think that just because it is a buyers' market they can take longer or offer lower; but no matter what the market is, the great homes that are priced correctly go very quickly—sometimes within 24 hours.

Presenting in the Negotiation of an Offer

Great real estate agents have the ability to negotiate a win/win situation for both the buyer and the seller. Some agents think if one wins the other has to lose, but with a little bit of skill, you can negotiate an offer that is a win for both.

When we are in negotiations on behalf of a client, we involve everyone in trying to come up with a win/win solution. We may say to the buyers, for example, "Help me out here. Help me understand how you arrived at that price. How can our sellers see this as a positive?" Or, in countering to the buyers we might say to our sellers, "Help me explain to the buyers how this may be of benefit to them."

We need to make sure that we, as agents, are not getting our own egos in the middle of the negotiations. We are there to represent the buyer or the seller, not to take it personally or make the decision for them. We have seen agents negotiate their buyers or sellers out of a really good deal because the agents have started taking it personally. You always want to have your clients' best interests at heart and get them the best deal that matches their needs. If you have accomplished that, then you have done your job.

We have discovered that a good strategy (sometimes) is to get both the buyers and the sellers in a room together when the situation warrants it. Most of the time, they will not react directly to the buyers (or sellers) the same way they would to their agents, and we have found that this is sometimes the only way to make the deal come together.

Negotiating is a give-and-take strategy, so you have to find out what is important to each side. We often say, "If we can get the buyers to do this, what would you be willing to do?" Ask great questions that will bring out what is most important to each side. "If we can get the price up, would you be willing to give a little on how quickly they can get into the home?" Most people are willing to be a little flexible if someone asks.

We tell our sellers, as well, that usually the first offer they get is the best offer. They often don't believe that, so we keep a repertoire of stories that substantiate that statement. Perhaps it may be about the sellers who decided not to take their first offer, and six months later the best offer they had was ten percent below that first one. We try to keep the situation light and often encourage our buyers not to be upset at the person who *made* the offer if it was too low because there were other people who went through their home and *didn't make* an offer at all. Or we may say, "You know, this offer is better than the one we had yesterday!" Then they will ask, "Oh, we had one yesterday?" "No, so this is better than the one we had yesterday." We try to keep them from getting emotional. Sometimes we may ask, "Would you buy this home at this price?" They may be expecting the buyer to pay a price that they themselves wouldn't even pay.

When you are negotiating with another agent, be sure not to say anything that you wouldn't say in front of your clients or give personal information you know they would not want you to divulge. If you wouldn't say it with them sitting in the room, it is probably not something you should be saying.

When we are negotiating for a buyer and the negotiations have stalled, we often ask our buyer, "If you don't get this home, how will you feel tomorrow when you wake up?" That usually motivates them to make their best offer. We often use the same tactic with our sellers: "If I tell you tomorrow that these buyers have bought another home, are you okay with that? What's your Plan B if this doesn't work out?" Again, people act more on what they self-discover than on what we tell them. We often tell them it is like a tennis match: "We always want to hit the ball back over the net. We never want to stop the negotiations when the ball is on our side of the net. We always want to give them one more opportunity to accept or reject our offer."

Remember, sometimes we assume what their needs are if we have not done a good job in doing a consultative presentation and assessing their needs. I was negotiating a very expensive home for someone one time, and he said to me, "Linda, I do not want to lose this house over $40,000!" I thought $40,000 was a lot of money; but obviously I had misunderstood his needs and expectations. That was a big "ah ha" for me—it is not my place to make a decision for my clients as to what they will or won't pay. So now we sometimes ask, "How are you going to feel if you lose this house over $20,000?" If you have really matched someone to the perfect home, price may not be an issue at all.

We had some friends visiting a few weeks ago who were negotiating on a house for $2.3 million, and they made an offer of $1.7 million. The owner came back with a full-price counter offer. There was obviously a lot of money on the table, but they knew it was the home they really wanted, and they didn't feel that it was worth losing the house over the difference!

We had a good real estate friend tell us once that, yes, we as real estate agents should know what the market value for the home is, but that it is not our decision to make whether our clients will pay more than market value for the home. She tells her buyers, "I'm going to tell you three times if I think there are some reasons (like price) that you shouldn't buy a home, and then I am going to take my commission." Basically, that's all you can do. Your job is to provide the information to your buyers and sellers and disclose everything you feel you need to disclose so you can help them make a wise decision. But you can't make their decision for them. You can tell them you think they are making a mistake (the highway is too busy, the resale will be too hard), but at the end of the day they get to decide.

Consultative Presentation to Sellers

I. Call received from sellers
    A. Listing Qualifier Form completed by staff
    B. Appointment set for listing agent to go to the home
    C. Pre-sale package sent to sellers

II. Listing agent's consultative presentation at the home
    A. Ask to sit at kitchen table
    B. Build rapport with sellers, using F-O-R-D
    C. Ask for sellers' expectations of meeting
    D. Discuss the three possible outcomes of the meeting
    E. Ask for sellers' needs and expectations in the sale of their home (for a "10" meeting, a 10-plus, and a 10-plus-plus)
    F. Clarify the priority of sellers' top three needs
    G. Tailor presentation toward sellers' needs (in order listed by seller)
        1. Discuss pricing
            a. Help sellers self-discover the appropriate price for their home
            b. Explain to clients how the market will accept or reject the price
        2. Discuss timing
        3. Discuss communication (ask for their media preference)
    H. Quickly review pre-sale package and marketing strategies
    I. Handle objections (have at least three responses ready for each objection)
        1. Commission
        2. Higher price quoted by another real estate agent
        3. Length of time for listing agreement
        4. Interviewing other agents
            a. Give them Interview Questions for other real estate agents
            b. Offer to cancel appointments with other real estate agents
    J. Close the sale
    K. Communicate, communicate, communicate
    L. Meet and exceed sellers' expectations

Consultative Presentation to Buyers

I. Call received from buyer
   A. Buyer Questionnaire Form completed by staff
   B. Call given to buyers' agent
      1. Ask buyers if they are working with another agent
      2. Ask buyers if they are first-time homeowners
      3. Schedule appointment for buyers to come into the office

II. Buyers' agent's consultative presentation in the office
   A. Give buyers a tour of the office
   B. Discuss the three possible outcomes of the meeting
   C. Have buyers complete the checklist that tells:
      1. How they came to know about your company
      2. How soon they need to buy a home
   D. Assess the buyers' level of motivation
   E. Give buyers the Agency Disclosure Form
   F. Discuss the Buyer Representation Form
      1. Discuss the benefits of buyer representation
      2. Ask the buyers to sign the agreement
   G. Educate the buyer on the current market
   H. Meet and exceed buyers' expectations

Important
P O I N T S

1. If you are going to be in the business of meeting and exceed-ing your clients' expectations, you have to find out what those expectations are.

2. You control the dynamics of the presentation. Leave your-self an out, and let the sellers know that you don't take every listing. If they have an unrealistic need or expectation in the sale of their home that you don't believe you could meet and exceed, it would be better to let them down at the beginning by not taking the listing than to disappoint them later.

3. Determine the sellers' top three needs and expectations by asking them to tell you what it would take to make the trans-action a 10, then a 10-plus, and then a 10-plus-plus. Then clarify the priority of those three needs to make sure you are on the same page with the seller, and design your presentation to address their needs.

4. A great agent tells clients what they need to hear, rather than what they themselves want to hear.

5. People will normally act on what they self-discover, rather than on what we tell them.

6. Help your clients to see the market as something you have to strategize together to beat—not something you (their real estate agents) are teaming up with against them.

7. Communication with the sellers after you get the listing is criti-cally important.

8. When you receive a call from buyers, a good goal should be to get them into your office and do a consultative presentation with them to assess their needs.

9. Assessing the buyers' level of motivation is a very important step because it lets you know how much time you should spend with the buyers.

10. Great real estate agents have the ability to negotiate a win/win situation for both the buyer and the seller.

6

How to Present at the Closing Table

No Surprises!

Early on in my career, I was closing a transaction for a family with three small children. They were buying a bank-owned property, which meant that there was no "heart" to which we could appeal on the other side of the transaction. The real estate agent who was handling the sale had no sense of urgency. To make matters worse, it was a holiday weekend, *and* it was a "domino" transaction—my buyers' were selling their home, and their buyers had to move in by the same day we were closing. So that meant my buyers had to move into the bank-owned home by that same day as well. They had nowhere else to go; they would have been out on the street if we did not close the transaction that day. My back-up plan (and I believe you should *always* have one) was to put them up in a hotel if we were not able to close before the holiday weekend. The morning of the closing, I could see that things were not happening fast enough to close by that afternoon. I discovered that the problem was with the lender, which was located in Houston, Texas. I flew to Houston, rented a car, drove to the bank, got the papers signed, brought them back to Denton, and took them to the title company. We funded that very afternoon, so my buyers could move into their home. Now, would they have been okay if they had stayed in a hotel? Sure. But at that emotional and stressful time in their lives, that is not what they wanted to do. It was very important to me to culminate the transaction and ensure that they were in their home before the holiday weekend.

The cornerstone of a successful real estate business is great closings! Those real estate agents who really take heart in making the closing a "happy ending" are the ones who make a big difference in this industry. Remember, it's not about the money—it's about meeting and exceeding people's needs. Strangely enough though, we have found that success follows when we operate our business with heart and strive to meet our clients' needs. The rest of the story is that the little family ended up buying and selling multiple homes with us throughout the years! We made a customer for life when we went above and beyond to meet their needs. We have also found that great closings generate raving fans that refer us to all of their friends and neighbors. Remember, the real estate business is a "contact sport." When clients experience the energy of great service, they *will* bring you more business from the people with whom they are in contact.

The closing is the most difficult—but most important—time of the transaction. If you are not prepared at the closing table, it will cost you. *The best time to ensure a smooth closing is while you are writing the contract.* Sales people are naturally optimistic. We real estate agents tend to write a contract as if everything will go well when in actuality we should write it with the worst-case scenario in mind. *Rarely ever does everything happen perfectly, and we should write the contract in such a way that all bases are covered.*

If real estate agents would write the contract with a heart for both sides—a heart for the buyer and a heart for the seller—many problems could be eliminated. *Closings are generally disastrous when agents write the contract in such a way that one party will win and the other will lose.* The closing is a very emotional time for buyers and sellers alike, and if either gets too stressed in the transaction, the whole deal could fall through. *Therefore, when we are writing a contract, we ask both parties to agree to a win/win situation.* That way, everyone is happy at the closing table.

We have found that there are several things to consider when writing a contract and preparing for a closing that will put everyone in a win/win position:

1. Make sure the price is agreeable to all parties.

2. Require a pre-approval letter from the buyers as opposed to a pre-qualification letter.

3. Choose a closing date other than the end of the month. The end of the month is like a major city freeway in rush hour—it is backed up solid and there is no room for dealing with any last-minute problems. Movers, real estate agents, mortgage companies, and title companies are swamped. It would be much easier on everyone to schedule the closing earlier in the month, even if it costs the seller a few days' interest.

4. Close on any day but Friday. If the sellers are buying another home and are not able to get their funding on Friday, it

would be Monday before they actually get their funding, and therefore would be Monday or after before they could move in.

5. Choose a mortgage company that is reputable, and one that will tell you *early on* when there is a problem—not on the day of closing!

6. Give a decent amount of time after closing and funding for possession. We recommend at least seven days, to allow room for error.

7. Schedule the final walk-through prior to the day of closing to allow time to correct any problems that may arise.

8. Ask for a sizeable amount of earnest money—enough to keep the buyers engaged when buyers' remorse kicks in.

9. Communicate, communicate, and communicate. *The closing is a very emotional time for buyers and sellers alike, and communication is absolutely critical.* At that point in the transaction, no news is bad news. Talk things through with your buyers or sellers before the closing so that they understand everything that will take place. Sometimes they agree to things up front, not realizing the consequences. In fact, we recommend making a list of everything that could go wrong in a transaction, so they will be prepared. *Make sure the sellers understand that the transaction is not complete until the money is in their hands; and recommend that they don't sign leases, schedule movers, or spend money on a new home until they are very confident that the sale will go through.* Even if they are not leasing or purchasing their new home from you, remind them that everything is contingent upon the sale *and* funding of their home. Remember, if their life gets stressful, your life gets stressful!

We have a Contract Manager who handles all of the closings in our office. I have often said that her appropriate title should be "Firefighter," complete with a firefighter's uniform and hat, since there are so many fires to put out during this part of the transaction. Because of the stress associated with closings, buyers and sellers alike often view them as life and death situations. The stress increases, and emotions come out! *In the real estate industry, a large number of properties fall out of contract and never make it to the closing table.* We have found that the only way to effectively reduce that percentage is to have a full-time, specialized staff person who concentrates 100 percent of their efforts toward getting properties to closing. **If you are an individual agent, we recommend that you hire someone for this position as quickly as possible.** If you are spending your own time focusing on these critical tasks to bring properties to closing, it is taking your valuable time away from prospecting and building your business.

Closing is a process, and not an event. It actually starts when you put the home under contract, and everything you do from that point forward should lead up to a positive closing. You want your clients to feel good about the purchase of their new home or the accomplishment of the sale, and nothing will kill their enthusiasm more than a last-minute hitch. The key to presenting well at the closing table is diligent preparation.

If a property falls out of contract, it is usually because of one of three reasons:

1. Financing can go awry if the buyers' credit is not up to the lenders' standards, if they had a bankruptcy that has not been cleared from the credit report, or if there is a condition required by underwriting that has not been met (payoff of a lien or credit card, etc.).

2. Negotiations can fall through on repairs if the buyers and sellers cannot come to an agreement on who will pay for what repairs.

3. Occasionally the title company finds something in the title search that cannot be reconciled.

It is very important to have a full system that goes into place when a home goes under contract—a system that ensures there will be no surprises at the closing table. Our system for getting homes we have sold to a successful closing includes:

1. When negotiations for the price of the home have been completed, the agent prepares a "Net Sheet" for the sellers, which shows the estimated amount of money they will make from the sale of their home. This estimation is based on information provided by the sellers (payoff on the home, etc.). Our agents tell the sellers in advance that there are generally only two numbers on the HUD statement they will receive at closing that could possibly contradict the Net Sheet and cause them to be unhappy: 1) If the payoff on their home was actually higher than the payoff amount the sellers provided; and 2) If there are taxes that are due that have not yet been paid. Both of these areas could cause the sellers' profit from the home to be lower than expected, and in order to ensure a smooth closing, it is very important to prepare them in advance.

2. The agent notifies the seller that the property is under contract. From this point to the actual day of closing, the Contract Manager is the main contact with the client, unless there is a problem in which she needs to involve the agent.

Of course, the agents are always available to answer questions or get involved if necessary.

3. The agent sends the contract and the earnest money to the title company. The title company "receipts" the contract and earnest money, sends the contract back to our Contract Manager, and then begins the title search on the property.

4. The Contract manager enters the following contract information into an Excel spreadsheet in the computer:
   a. Date of closing
   b. Property Address
   c. Amount of commission
   d. Transaction fee
   e. Commission split
   f. Referral information, if applicable
   g. Mortgage company
   h. Title company
   i. Number of days on market
   j. Sales price
   k. Listing Agent

5. The Contract Manager enters the following information onto a checklist that will help her keep track of tasks and deadlines:
   a. Name of sellers
   b. Name of buyers
   c. Property address
   d. Listing Agent
   e. Buyers' Agent
   f. Mortgage company
   g. Title company
   h. Option period deadline

    i. Date of inspection (After the Buyers' Agent schedules the inspection, the Inspector calls our Contract Manager. If she has not heard from an Inspector in a reasonable amount of time before the option period ends, she calls the Buyers' Agent to see when the inspection is scheduled. Our Contract Manager then notifies the sellers of the date of the inspection.)

    j. Date of appraisal (The appraisal is usually done at least a week before closing. The buyers pay for the appraisal, and they usually like to wait until their financing is secured and repairs are completed. The Contract Manager makes sure the appraisal is completed in a timely manner prior to closing.)

    k. Financing deadline

6. The Contract Manager enters the following information into Online Agent, computer software that shows the status of the property:

    a. Property address

    b. Date of contract

    c. Date of closing

    d. Contact information on buyers and sellers

    e. Mortgage company

    f. Commission split

    g. Status ("Opted," at this point, showing the property is in the option period for the time stipulated in the contract, usually 7, 10 or 15 days. During the option period, the inspection is completed and negotiations are completed for the repairs. Buyers can still opt out of the contract during this time if negotiations fall through, so it is important to facilitate getting the inspection done and sensitively fostering cooperation between both parties during the option period.)

7. The Contract Manager enters the following information on a Commission Disbursement form:
   a. Name of seller
   b. Name of buyer
   c. Mortgage company
   d. Name of both agents
   e. Contract date
   f. Closing date
   g. Commission split and commission totals
   h. Referral disbursement, if applicable
   i. Total to be paid to real estate company

   This form is given to the office manager, who transfers the disbursement information to another form (a Commission Disbursement Authorization (CDA) Form) to be faxed to the title company. Just prior to closing, the title company will write the disbursement checks. At this time our company cuts checks to the broker and the agents. Check with your company, some don't allow checks to be cut directly to the agent.

8. A letter is sent from our Contract Manager to our sellers outlining the steps to be followed during the option period and up to closing, including the deadlines involved. Remember, this is a high-emotion time, and communication is *crucial* at this point of the transaction. The more information you can give the clients, the better! We have included in the Appendix a copy of a sample letter to sellers, and you can also go to the website www.PresentationMasteryforRealtors.com to find that, as well as a sample letter to buyers, which suggests to the buyers when to have their utilities turned on (a list of area utility companies is attached to the letter) and when to transfer their mail. The letter also gives information about

homeowners' insurance, closing funds, the walk-through, homestead exemption, and state laws regarding new car and driver's license in case they are new to the state.

9. The Contract Manager makes personal contact with the sellers by phone to answer any questions they may have. At this point, she encourages the sellers not to schedule movers or spend any money on their new home until after the option period has ended.

10. The Contract Manager calls the buyers' agent to get the date for the inspection and the name of the buyers' lender, so she can ensure that the buyers have met their financing deadlines. If she sees that the deadlines are not being met, she notifies the sellers that there could be a delay. Financing can be a major "hiccup," so it is very important to monitor that activity.

11. If the seller does not already have a survey on the property, the Contract Manager orders a survey. (Laws regarding surveys vary from state to state, but a survey is required in Texas.)

12. The Contract Manager stays in constant contact with the buyer's agent regarding any repairs that are required on the home. She assures the sellers that they have the option of paying for some or all of the repairs themselves or they can negotiate any or all of the repairs. She ensures that prior to the end of the option period all parties have come to an agreement on the repairs and have signed the amendment stating such an agreement has been reached. She also sends a copy of the amendment to the sellers and to the title company, and she puts a copy in her file.

13. Once the option period is over, the status of the property is changed in Online Agent to "Contract Pending." She

also sees that a "Contract Pending" rider is added to the "For Sale" sign in the yard of the property. Once the option period is over, the only reason the property would not close would be the failure of the buyers to get financing within the stated time.

14. The Contract Manager stays in contact with the lenders and the buyers' agent on a regular basis to ensure things are progressing favorably. The lender will tell her when the loan is in underwriting, when it has been approved by underwriting, if there are conditions that have to be met, etc. She also stays in contact with the sellers (daily, if they prefer) to inform them of the progress or any problems that may arise.

15. The week before the scheduled closing, the Contract Manager:
    a. Checks the file to ensure all necessary amendments have been executed and received, and to make sure all repairs have been done.
    b. Calls the buyers' agent to see if there are any problems.
    c. Calls the lender to make sure the financing is on track.
    d. Calls the seller to answer questions and stays in touch with them daily until closing.
    e. Schedules the closing with the title company at least three days before, if possible. It's important to be fairly sure the lenders will have the closing documents ready by the scheduled date of closing. It is not unusual for the closing to be delayed because the documents have not been received from the lender, so the Contract Manager stays in constant contact with the lender to determine when the documents will be completed.

16. The Contract Manager schedules a walk-through of the home for the buyer and the buyers' agent, preferably the

day before closing, to ensure that all repairs are done and the home is in good order. If it is an FHA loan, the repairs may be required by the lender, and the inspector must come back out to make sure the repairs are done.

17. The title company prepares the HUD statement and sends it to the lender for approval. Ideally, the HUD statement will be sent to the Contract Manager in advance of closing and faxed to the sellers for review, but that does not always happen. If she does receive the HUD in advance, she checks it against her copy of the Net Sheet the agent gave to the sellers. If there are discrepancies, she calls the agent to determine the reason. If the difference cannot be reconciled, she calls the title company to find out why there is a discrepancy. Once she determines that the HUD is correct, she will call the sellers to discuss any differences.

18. The documents are signed by all parties at the closing. Most of the time the sellers' agent will go to closing. On rare occasions, the Contract Manager will go in the agent's place.

19. Once the money is transferred from the lender to the title company, the title company issues checks to the appropriate parties. The commission checks are sent to our Contract Manager, who makes sure they are accurate.

Now you understand why we call our Contract Manager "the Fireman!" She manages the entire closing process and makes it go as smoothly as possible. When we hired our Contract Manager, we made sure she was "behaviorally right" for the job (i.e., that her behavior and personality fit the profile required for this position). Generally, real estate agents themselves are more people-oriented than detail-oriented and are not as suited for taking care of the myriad of details that closings involve.

We send a questionnaire out to our sellers and buyers after each closing asking them to rate our services (more on this in Chapter Seven). Generally, the person they remember most in the closing process is our Contract Manager, and most clients lavish appreciation for her assistance. It's very difficult for these people to go through this very intense process, most of which they have no control over, and they appreciate the fact that she is there to answer questions, handle potential problems, and communicate everything that is going on during the process.

Whether you handle closings yourself or have an assistant to help you, you need a great system to keep you on track during the process. And remember, constant communication with your clients is *essential!*

VERY Important POINTS

1. The cornerstone of a successful real estate business is great closings.

2. The best time to ensure a smooth closing is while you are writing the contract. Rarely does everything happen perfectly, and you should write the contract in such a way that all bases are covered.

3. When you are writing a contract, ask both parties to agree to a win/win situation.

4. The closing is a very emotional time for buyers and sellers alike, and communication is absolutely critical.

5. Make sure the sellers understand that the transaction is not complete until the money is in their hands and recommend that they don't sign leases, schedule movers, or spend money on a new home until they are very confident that the sale will go through.

6. In the real estate industry, a large number of properties fall out of contract and never make it to the closing table. The best way to effectively reduce that percentage is to have a full-time, specialized staff person who concentrates 100 percent of his or her efforts toward getting properties to closing.

7. It's very important to have a complete system that goes into place when a home goes under contract—a system that ensures there will be no surprises at the closing table.

Presenting
After the Sale

Building a Referral-Based Business

"I have a referral for your parents," the PTA mom told our daughter Bailey at school one day. "Why don't you just give it to me, and I'll give it to them," Bailey said. "Oh, no! I'll call their office," the mom responded. Apparently we had trained her well. So many times, people had given our name to one of their friends or family and told them to call us, but we never heard from them. *So we learned over the years to train our clients to call us directly and give us the referral name, so we can contact them! Then we immediately reward the person who gave us the referral.*

At least once a year we emphasize our Referral Reward Program by mailing out postcards to everyone in our database for three months

143

in a row, thanking them for their past business and reminding them of our Referral Reward Program. As a reward for each referral (whether they actually do business with us or not), we send the person who gives us the referral a $25 gift certificate to a local establishment—a hair salon or spa, a restaurant, a movie theater, etc.—and their name is entered into a drawing at the end of the year for a trip. *We reward them whether their referral does business with us or not because what we are actually doing is rewarding loyalty in our clients—for their own business and for the business they refer to us.* This program is a very effective way to build our referral business, which is one reason our business has been so successful. Because we provide great service, reward for referrals, and communicate with our clients on a regular basis after the closing, about 75 percent of our business is repeat and referrals.

Real estate agents dream clients are those who stay with them for a lifetime of real estate needs and refer them to all of their friends and family. Presenting effectively to the client during and after the sale establishes that kind of relationship. Again, the secret is in the system. Just as we have a system for taking a property from contract to closing, we have another system for effectively communicating with our clients after the closing.

After the property closes, funding has been completed, and all disbursement checks have been reviewed for accuracy, the Contract Manager in our office turns over the property file and the checks to our Operations and Marketing Director (office manager) whose full-time responsibility is maintaining a constant relationship with our vast amount of past clients. Keep in mind that it has taken us years to get to this point, but the sooner you can get there, the more referrals and repeat business you will get. Here is her system, which kicks in after the closing of a property:

1. Deposit the checks for the company's portion of the commission.

2. Complete the forms to be turned into our franchise organization in accordance with our franchise agreement.

3. If the sold property was one of our listings:
   a. Close it out in MLS
   b. Send an e-mail to everyone on our staff to let them know the property is no longer on the market
   c. Pull the property off of our website
   d. Order a "Sold" postcard to be sent out to 300—500 homes surrounding the property to let the homeowners know we sold a property in their neighborhood (and that we can sell theirs as well). We get addresses for these cards through mail houses, listed in the local yellow pages under "Mailing Services." If your phone book does not list that category, you can call print shops listed under "Printing Services" and ask them if they have access to mailing lists or if they can refer you to someone who does. We prefer to outsource this project to one company that does everything—prints the cards, provides the mailing lists, affixes the mailing labels, and mails the cards. Our total cost per card, including postage, is 60 cents. Another option, which is less expensive but much more work, is to get the addresses from the tax records at the county courthouse. Be sure to always have one card addressed to your office, so you will know when it hits the market.
   e. Send a letter to the clients, asking them to complete a survey questionnaire to rate our services. A self-addressed

return envelope is included with the letter. Approximately 20 percent of our clients return these surveys.

f. Send a survey letter to the co-agent in the transaction to get his or her feedback on whether it was a positive experience. That return envelope is addressed to our operating partner who handles the listing specialists.

g. Print out a letter to the clients to be mailed in January, which includes a copy of the HUD Statement for their tax preparation. These letters are placed in a box, where they are held until January.

h. Print out a letter to be placed in a tickler file and mailed out on the one-year anniversary of the sale or purchase of the clients' home. This letter asks the client to remember us for their real estate needs and asks for referrals.

i. If the client was referred by another agent, she sends a thank-you letter to that agent, along with the referral check and a copy of the HUD statement.

4. When one of our listings is sold by an agent from a different company, our Operations and Marketing Director sends out an "orphan" letter to the buyers, congratulating them on the purchase of their new home and offering to be of assistance in any way we can. Statistics tell us that other agents do not usually communicate with their clients after the sale. Since the listing was ours, we are the most qualified to answer any questions they may have about the property, and since the other agent probably will not stay in touch with them, we stand a good chance of getting them as a client for their future real estate needs.

5. She enters the buyers and sellers (including the "orphan" clients) into our database.

Once you put clients in your database, immediately start them on your "33 Touch Program." This program is the most effective way to get referrals. Gary Keller introduced the "33 Touch Program" in his book, *The Millionaire Real Estate Agent*. We have adapted it for our business (we usually make around 25 touches, or contacts, a year), which has turned into a very profitable practice. Here are some of the ways we contact the over 4,000 clients in our database each year (examples are included in the Appendix):

1. In January we mail out an informational flyer explaining the Texas Homestead Exemption and how to file for it, and we attach a Homestead Exemption form.

2. In April, we send a postcard to our clients offering free assistance in protesting their property taxes if they think the increases are incorrect or unfair. (The Central Appraisal District mails out their property tax letters in May.)

3. At the end of June, we send out a postcard announcing 4th of July events that are being held in the community.

4. We send out postcards announcing our Referral Reward Program for three months in a row (usually in late spring or summer).

5. In August, we send out a postcard outlining Back-to-School Safety Tips for parents to teach their children who ride the bus or who walk or ride their bikes to school.

6. In October, we send out a postcard reminding our clients of three things: to set their clocks back for the time change, to keep their calendar holders for the next year's refill, and how to get a complimentary market evaluation of their home.

7. In November, we mail a postcard to past clients inviting them to bring their children into our office on a set date near the end of the month to have a complimentary picture made with Santa. We ask them to bring a canned good to support area food banks.

8. In December, we send out calendar refills (with a holder for new clients) and a Christmas letter. The calendars are 8½ by 11-inch size, with one page per month, and the holders are magnetic. Our clients love these!

We also send out postcards when something in the news touches the real estate industry, such as the anticipated rise of interest rates, to let our clients know that now is a good time to buy. We ask for referrals on several of the pieces (including our calendar), but *each "touch" is a reminder to our clients that we are there to fulfill any real estate needs for them or their family or friends.* The funny thing is we are in such constant contact with the people in our database that often our "orphan" clients forget that we were not the ones who sold them their home!

It doesn't necessarily take 33 touches through direct contact, just as long as your name and face are in front of your clients on a regular basis. We do an incredible amount of advertising. Three Sundays out of each month, we run a full-page, full-color ad on the back page of the real estate section of our local newspaper. And we run a full-page, full-color ad on the back page of the local homes magazine that comes out once a month in our local Sunday paper. Our brand is all over our vehicles and yard signs as well.

Just remember that every touch you make with your past clients leads you one step closer to another referral. *You cannot build a real estate business without referrals. The more touches you make, the stronger your referral base will be.*

Important POINTS

1. Train your clients to call you directly and give you the referral name, so you can contact the referral directly. Then immediately reward the person who gave you the referral.

2. Reward for the referral whether or not it actually results in business because what you are actually doing is rewarding loyalty in your clients—for their own business and for the business they refer to you.

3. A real estate agents dream clients are those who stay with them for a lifetime of real estate needs and refer them to all of their friends and family. Presenting effectively to the client after the sale establishes that kind of relationship.

4. Once you put clients in your database, immediately start them on your "33 Touch Program." Each "touch" is a reminder to your clients that you are there to fulfill any real estate needs for them or their family or friends.

5. You cannot build a strong real estate business without referrals. The more touches you make, the stronger your referral base will be.

THREE

Building Relationships Through Presentation Mastery

Your Allied Resources

Our client was laughing as he greeted us at the door. "You're not going to believe the phone call I just had," he said. "Here you are, driving up—*in a limo*—to pick us up and take us to dinner, and I just got chewed out by another agent for giving you my business!" To be fair, the other real estate agent *was* one that his father had done business with for 20 years, but no one in the family had ever gone to dinner with her in a limo! This client and his two siblings had inherited millions of dollars worth of property from their father. They chose three real estate agents in our area (including the McKissack Group and the agent with whom their father had always done business) and divided up the listings among us.

Whoever successfully closed their properties was given the listings from the other real estate agents as they expired. In the end, we got most of the listings. As we neared the closing on the last property with them, we rented a limo and took all three siblings and their spouses, along with our Closing Coordinator and her husband to a very nice dinner. Jim had sold a property for this client in the past and had identified him as an allied resource. Jim began to nurture the relationship, and that's why we were among the three real estate companies chosen to participate in the sale of all of this property. The client became one of our best advocates and sent a lot of business our way over the years.

As your database grows, it will include two groups of people: your sphere of influence and your allied resources. When I first got into the business, I thought if I got a person into my sphere of influence I had a client for life. I just knew that if I had a database of 300, they would all be my raving fans and do business with me and no one else. Not so. The first time I went by the home of someone with whom I had discussed real estate needs and saw another real estate agents sign in their yard, I was devastated. I would guess that everyone who sells houses has experienced the same scenario. Rather than getting distressed when that happens, you need to understand that *just because someone is in your sphere of influence, it doesn't mean they will always do business with you.*

Actually, very few in your database will move from your sphere of influence group into your allied resource group—those people who know you, love you, and would never dream of doing business with anyone else. Your allied resources are your best promoters and your best source of referrals. They try to influence everyone they know to do business with you. In reality, you may never have more than five to fifteen allied resources in your career, but you don't really need very many. With no more than a few, you can build an extremely successful real estate business.

If you have not yet identified those in your allied resource group, look through your database. They are probably already in your sphere of influence, and you just have not recognized them. Those people in your database who have these three characteristics are probably your allied resources:

1. They don't mind if you make money. They want you to be successful.
2. Their names have come up repeatedly as those who have referred business to you.
3. They are in professional leadership rolls with access to a lot of people, and they use their influence to send people your direction.

We went for many years not understanding what an allied resource was or how to figure out who ours were. We had a client appreciation party one year, and I called a real estate agent friend and told her I wanted to acknowledge at the party the handful of people whom we knew had given us a lot of business over the years. The only problem was, I had no way of knowing who they were because we had not kept good records. I wanted to brainstorm with her and get some ideas as to how to do that. She suggested we simply ask them. That was the big client appreciation party at which we had brought in a professional photographer to take pictures of the clients and their families with Andy, the leader of the 1950s and 1960s band who had a wild and crazy "comb" hairdo. (We knew the pictures would be great conversation pieces—and that our name would come up over and over again as a result.) The clients had to fill out a form so we could mail the pictures to them. My agent friend suggested that we include a question on that form: How many referrals do you think you have given the McKissack Group over the past 12 months? With just that little maneuver, we were able to narrow down our allied resources to about 10 people. We recognized them in front of the whole group at the party that very evening, thanked them, and gave them a gift certificate to a local restaurant. So even if you have not kept records and identified your allied resources in the past, now is a great time to start. You can simply send out a survey to your database and ask them how many referrals they have given you over the past 12 months.

Once you identify your allied resources, it is very important to nurture and build those relationships. Successfully presenting yourself and your business to your allied resources will yield incredible results. Start socializing with them; put them on the top of your list to call on a regular basis—weekly, or at least monthly; ask them for advice ("I would love your opinion on this matter."); assist them in their business however you can (referrals, etc.); and seek ways to provide added value services to help them improve their lives. Include these people in your life. Spend time with them either face-to-face or on the phone as often as possible. Create an intimate relationship with them—one that both you and they will cherish. *And, above all, always show them how grateful you are for the business they send your way!*

Train your allied resources how to give you referrals. As we discussed in Chapter Six, we have found that it works best if people will call us with referrals rather than asking the person being referred to call us. Your allied resources are going to be continually promoting your business, so be sure they know how you prefer to receive referrals.

Before we identified our allied resources, we actually let a great one get away. She was an interior decorator and we did not pay close attention to how much business she sent our way. We failed to nurture that relationship and give back to it, and we lost her. She and a builder friend probably sent us more business than anyone else during that period of our business. Thank goodness, we recognized the builder as an allied resource before we lost him, and he continues to send us a lot of business today.

Among your allied resources as in any other group you will still see the 80/20 rule in play—probably 20 percent of them will send you 80 percent of your referrals, and the other 80 percent will only send you a few here and there. But they are all important, and it is wise to nurture the relationship with all of them.

VERY Important POINTS

1. Just because someone is in your sphere of influence it doesn't mean they will always do business with you.

2. Very few in your database will move from your sphere of influence group into your allied resource group—those people who know you, love you, and would never dream of doing business with anyone else.

3. In reality you may have only five to 15 allied resources in your career, but you don't really need very many. With no more than a few, you can build an extremely successful real estate business.

4. Once you identify your allied resources, it is very important to nurture and build those relationships. Always show them how grateful you are for the business they send your way!

5. Successfully presenting yourself and your business to your allied resources will yield incredible results.

6. Train your allied resources how to give you referrals.

Your Relationships

The people with whom you align yourself and your business have a dramatic impact on shaping your future. Your relationships with your broker, your clients, other real estate agents, your outside resources, and your family are all very important, and the success of those relationships will ultimately determine your level of success in the real estate business.

Your Broker

One of the most vital relationships you will enter will be the company for whom you work. Use extreme caution and wisdom when you are considering what broker with whom to associate.

Our premise that "life is a series of presentations" is actually a two-way street. As you begin to choose the company you'll entrust your future for a period of time, it's very important to carefully observe the presentations being made as you interview them.

We can't stress enough the importance of choosing this relationship with care. Listen carefully to their presentations and discern what they are really saying. It can be very expensive to change brokers, so you need to make the right choice on the front end if at all possible. When you are in the process of selecting the broker with whom you want to partner, we encourage you to diligently pursue the answers to these questions:

- Will this broker encourage me to be the best I can be and grow to the highest level I can grow? Will the broker support me to be the brand or will the broker's company be the brand over me?
- Does the company have a strong commitment to education *and* business training?
- Does the company allow me to use my own phone number?
- Is the company growing?
- What is the value proposition (i.e., what are the economics and commission splits)? Is there a cap amount on royalties and commissions or are you paying the broker all year?
- Is this broker's vision larger than mine? When your vision is larger than the broker's, you are working for the wrong company.
- What is the broker's exit strategy? Who owns the listings if I should leave—me or the broker? The day we left our last broker to go with our current franchise organization, we had 52 listings, and those listings all belonged to our dependent broker. Somehow, I had missed this point when I signed the contract to go with that broker. (The good news is that within a week

and a half, most of those sellers had said they would only do business with me and demanded to change their listings.) Leaving a company is usually a very emotional and stressful time, especially if you have poured years of your heart and soul into that business. We were told that day to turn in our keys and leave by 5 P.M. That is not how you want a five-year relationship to end! And you certainly don't want to add to that the stress of losing all of your listings.

One of the most valuable pearls of advice we can give you is to mentally picture your life 10 years from now with the broker you are considering. Imagine what your life will look like after being with this broker for ten years. A good way to do this is to find someone in the office who has been with the company for ten or more years and see what his or her life is like. I spent five years with a company early in my career, and the owner for whom I worked was a very nice lady. I finally realized, however, that no matter how long I worked for her, I would always be at the same place in my career. There would never be a bigger opportunity with that company than the one I had already accomplished. If you can't look up and see that next opportunity with your company—that next big goal to accomplish—your success will be very limited.

Often, real estate agents don't even realize they should have expectations for their relationship with their broker. They don't know to shop around. They understand that the broker has the right to say, "Here's what I expect from you," but they don't think to ask what they have the right to expect from the broker. Many times this imbalance results in great dissatisfaction over the years, but because they don't have a standard with which to evaluate the relationship, they don't understand why they are discontented. When I selected my first broker, I went with one who owned a fish restaurant we frequented on the weekends. What a way to select a broker! I stayed with her for six months and got no training whatsoever. I literally had to go to the health club with her at five in the morning just to pick her brain and learn what I could about selling real estate! She was a great lady, but it was just not a wise choice for me.

Even when I chose my second broker, I chose the company because it offered two whole weeks of training on the front end! If I had only known then what I know now: *Education is a process, not an event. It is very important to find a company that has ongoing training that offers the next level of education as you grow as an agent.* In fact, we suggest that when you interview with a broker, you ask to see his monthly training calendar. If the broker does not have one with a minimum of six training days a week, turn around and walk out the door!

Your Clients

Your clients are the very lifeblood of your real estate business. Your relationships with them should be built on trust, honesty, and commitment to adding value to their lives and to the transaction. Even though we've already talked a lot about clients in this book, there are several things we must emphasize in this chapter about your relationship with your clients:

- It is simply out of the question to provide anything less than great customer service to your clients. Our society today is filled with people who make promises they don't fulfill. Your clients need to see that you are committed to exceeding their expectations. We look at it this way: if you go to a restaurant ten times and get great food and service every time, you may tell a friend or two about it. But if you go one time and the food or service is terrible, you will probably tell everyone you know about it! We want our clients to tell everyone they know about us, so we make it a point to provide the most excellent service in our marketplace.

- Communicate, communicate, communicate! I think we can safely say that there is no such thing as over-communication with a client during a transaction! The more you keep them in the loop, answer their questions, and calm their fears, the happier your clients will be when the transaction is complete. Happy clients translate into repeat clients and referrals.

- Money should never be more important than your client's needs. Be prepared to walk away from a commission if you believe the sale is not in their best interest. I have gone on several appointments over the years and discovered that the people had no business listing their home under their present circumstances. Rather than telling them what they wanted to hear in order to get the commission, I would spend fifteen or twenty minutes listening to their issues and then give them the best advice I knew to give, even if it had nothing to do with my making a commission. I truly believe that the bottom line of our success is that we have always tried to do the right thing for each person.

Other Real Estate Agents

A crucial relationship in this industry that has suffered for many years is that of agent to agent. You'll do more business with your peers than you will ever do with your clients, and other real estate agent relationships should be nurtured. I have watched agents deal very harshly with each other without realizing that those are the relationships that should be highly valued. *In actuality, real estate agents should treat each other with the utmost respect and even commit to helping each other.* Though one agent may represent the buyer and one the seller in a transaction, they are both pursuing the same goal—to be a conduit to make the transaction successful for the clients. The very best way to accomplish that is for the real estate agents to work together as a team in a mutually respectful relationship. After all, these other real estate agents are people you are going to do business with for the next 20 or 30 years! You will find that the people who are the most successful in this business are those who don't burn their bridges with other agents.

In order to be affiliated with Keller Williams in a franchise ownership role, one of the things we look for are owners who have influence with their peers within the industry. When we tour the country opening offices for Keller Williams, we have looked for people with not only high production but with a high level of influence as well. When these people get on the phone with other agents, they must be able to command enough respect both because of high production and because of their influence within the industry for those real estate agents to listen to what they have to say.

There are two things to remember when considering your relationship with others in your industry:

1. Don't burn your bridges. We need other people in order to be successful.
2. There are always people who have succeeded at a higher level than you have. Seek them out and benchmark them. Ask them to help you raise your level of success. But don't forget to help those who are coming up behind you. *It would be so much better if all real estate agents would look at the industry through an "abundance" mentality instead of a "scarcity" mentality. There is enough business out there for all of us! You don't have to lose for me to win, and vice versa; we both can win!*

Real estate professionals have to start focusing on the value of connecting with each other, and leveraging the relationships we build within the industry. Other industries work together, refer each other business, and team up to make sales happen. The top real estate agents figure out how to see value in each other and nurture our relationships just as much as they do any of their other relationships. We have seen creative players criticized rather than applauded when those doing the criticizing could have benefited greatly by just sitting down with those who were blazing the trail and asking them to talk about their ideas.

Your Affiliate Relationships

Years ago, title companies, mortgage companies, and builders would work to build relationships with real estate agents by taking them to lunch, bringing them doughnuts, and "courting" them in other ways. Probably one of the best things a title company ever did for us was to pay for our way to a seminar in California when I first got into the business. That seminar was the one that changed our entire paradigm about real estate and determined our whole course in the way we would operate our business.

As a result, we have had more of a "beholden" relationship with our affiliates, and it's one in which we have tried to add value to their lives and businesses just as they have to ours. And the good thing is that over the years, we have watched that relationship between real estate agents and their affiliates change industry-wide to more of a partnership—one in which they are mutually committed to helping each other grow.

A great agent/builder relationship can be extremely successful for both parties. Real estate agents can enhance that relationship by sitting down with both custom and volume builders and trying to understand their needs (like how much money the custom builder loses every day he has a house sitting empty). Often though, real estate agents don't understand how that relationship can benefit them especially in the case of builders who have their own on-site sales people. However, if agents will go out and build great relationships with the on-site sales people, they will soon be very comfortable with taking clients to see those builders' homes. Once the client is registered with the builder, the on-site sales person takes over the sale from there and the real estate agents' job just gets easier! The agent gets a commission for bringing the client to their office. It's a win/win situation. We have learned to take all of our clients to see the new construction homes because chances are they will wander out there anyway, and we want to be the ones to introduce them to the on-site sales people. We explain to our clients that the best way we can educate them about the market is to show them the whole market, so we recommend that they at least take a look at the new homes. We even make it easier for the builders by leasing a cubbyhole to them in the New Home Sales Center in our office where our clients can look at information on the builders' new homes before they go out.

We started our guaranteed sale program because it was a way for us to help the builders when they had clients who had a home to sell before they could buy a new home. Most on-site sales people don't really like to write contingency contracts, so this is a way to guarantee that the clients' homes will be sold by the time they are ready to close on their new home. But again, it's a win/win situation. The on-site sales people actually send the clients to us, and we get the commission on the new home they purchase!

In our Indianapolis office, we have found a way to enhance our relationship even further with the builders. Each month we bring all of our agents to one of the builders' model homes for a book club meeting where we review a book that helps the agents with their real estate business. (Our first book was *The Millionaire Real Estate Agent* by Gary Keller. We plan to review *Presentation Mastery for Realtors* at one of our future meetings!) We accomplish several objectives by doing this:

- Developing a relationship between the builders and the agents
- Driving traffic to the builders' homes
- Exposing the builders to our company and the benefits of doing business with us
- Teaching our agents valuable information about the real estate business through the book reviews

Both of these programs create win/win situations. They serve to put the builders and the agents on the same side instead of opposing sides. Builders are excellent sources of leads through our guaranteed sale program and our agents are great sources of buyers for the builders. Their traffic comes off of mass marketing that we could never afford to do. Our traffic comes from the many different sources of leads we pursue.

There are several things builders often do to strengthen their relationships with agents. Besides educating the agents about their homes, they sometimes bring in attorneys or other professionals to train the agents in real estate matters. And those who are really astute know that if they build a relationship with the top agents in the area and provide leads to them, they create a connection that will greatly benefit them in the long run. Those agents in turn will keep a steady stream of traffic coming their way.

A good title company and a good mortgage company may be the best partners you can have, either as a new agent or as a more experienced agent because their goals so closely resemble yours. Their hope, of course, is that as they help you build your business, you will automatically help them build theirs. We suggest that you find a title company and a mortgage company that have the same values you have, then sit down with each of the owners and say, "I want to create a partnership that benefits both of us." Then find things you can do together that will actually generate more business for both of you. Look for ways to help grow each other's businesses. It's an important part of building relationships.

Your Family

Your family is the most important relationship you have, and it is the one you need to nurture and protect more than any other. In reality, your family is usually the ultimate reason most people identify for building their real estate business. Whenever we talk to people who are struggling in this business and ask them what *end result* they desire from it, they almost always say something about their families.

Like any business, there will be aspects of this business that are not your favorite things to do. For many real estate agents, prospecting is one of them. But even though prospecting (or making calls or any other activity) may be hard for you, you want to ask yourself what it will *deliver* for you. If you are like most, it will ultimately have something to do with your family. When prospecting becomes hard and you don't want to do it, you need to remember that you are building this business so you can provide things for your family. It may be that your daughter wants to go to a very expensive college, or you want to put your children in private school. Or, it may be something more basic, like pulling your family once and for all out of financial distress. Again, it's a matter of making your best presentation to that audience of one—yourself—to convince yourself to do whatever it takes. Don't violate your relationship with your family because you don't want to do the hard things it takes to make you successful in this business.

When real estate agents first get into the business, they usually need money; but often what they really need is more time. *You can't manufacture more hours in each day, so you need to learn very quickly how to be extremely efficient with your time so you can spend more of it with your family.* Whether you are a new or a seasoned agent, you must learn to ask yourself this question when making decisions about where to spend your time: "If I say yes to this, what am I saying no to?" If you say yes to spending ten hours a day at the office, what are you saying no to? Not putting your child to bed? Not being there for your child's ball game or recital? Probably none of us would actually choose to miss out on those things, and remembering to ask that question helps clarify our priorities. On the other hand, you may be saying yes to spending time working with an unqualified buyer, which means you are saying no to working with qualified buyers and ultimately spending more time with your family. You may need to pick up the phone and make those five extra calls instead of spending more time with that unqualified buyer. One of the first things in this business you need to say yes to is learning to ask the right qualifying questions to buyers and sellers. There is nothing worse than finding yourself out on a listing call at 10:00 at night and realizing that you have just spent the evening with someone who is not qualified or motivated. Because you said no to learning to ask the right questions, you said yes to missing an entire evening with your family. If you don't stop to ask yourself what you are saying yes and no to, it may take you longer to see the full implication of the choices you are making.

That being said, however, there is both good news and bad news for those agents who are just starting their real estate careers. The bad news is that, as in any other business, much more of your time, energy, and resources are going to be required on the front end when you are building your business. *It is crucial that you pull your family together and explain to them that you are starting a new business and that you will be working a lot of hours and spending more time away from home—in the beginning.* For the record, the real estate business is very time-consuming. The hours you will spend away from your family, along with financial risk that you create in the beginning, *can* create stress. The successful agents, though, are those who are willing to find the right balance in their lives and then do whatever it takes on the front end to build a thriving career.

Now for the good news: *As you become more successful and build your referral and allied resource database, you'll learn how to better manage and leverage your time.* You will be able to choose the clients with whom you want to work, and your clients will learn to work with you on your terms. You won't be a slave to the client. In the beginning, when you don't have any credibility, you are willing to do a lot of things you wouldn't think of doing later on. As you grow, you will get control of your business. And as you increase your knowledge and your value proposition (your clients' realization of the value of working with you versus working with other agents), your independence will increase. At this point in our business, we have built such a high value proposition with our clients and they see such validity in what we do that they will work around our schedule in order to work with us. But in the beginning it was not like that.

One of the major problems real estate agents and other small business owners face is bringing their work home with them. They may find themselves bringing home the stress from the day and taking it out on the family, or staying on the phone all evening with business associates or clients.

We've found various ways to help us switch channels when we go home. Setting boundaries and turning off the cell phone at night has made a huge difference in our lives. Before we learned to switch channels, our children were saying things like, "I hate that telephone," or "I hate it when all you talk about is real estate." We also took our home telephone number off of our cards. If you give your number out, you *will* receive calls at home. Also, sometimes in the beginning I would feel guilty because I didn't always work when I was at work, and I would try to make up for it by working at home. When you are at work, work; when you are at home, be at home—both mentally and physically! That means you have to learn to be more efficient in both places!

We have also found that our children buy into our "real estate schedule" more if we let each of them pick a reward. We explain that this particular project we are working on now may take us away from home a little bit more; but that when we complete it, we will have accomplished a big goal. And we ask them what they would like as a reward when that happens for the sacrifice they made in allowing us to spend the time doing it. That way, when we walk in the door in the evening, we hear things like, "Did you get those calls made?" or "Did you get that new listing?" All of a sudden they are involved in and excited about what you are doing. We have found that agents who are having issues in their families usually also have issues in their businesses, and vice versa. It is so very important to focus on and nurture your relationship with your family. The reality is, your personal life has to be in order before you can succeed at the highest level. You have to respect the fact that they work together.

The bottom line is, if you are struggling in this business, you have not yet defined your basic reason for entering the business. The same could be true for any business, but the point is that it's important to define why you are doing what you're doing! More often than not it has something to do with your family.

In surveys of 80 and 90-year olds, none of them have said they wished they had worked more; most of them say they wish they had spent more time with their families. One of the things we love to do is to take my family and Jim's family on vacations. Years ago, my sister asked me why I couldn't be happy just being at home and being "normal." But after we flew her first class to Hawaii a few years ago, she started saying things like, "Would you like for me to come and help with the kids, so you can do whatever it is you do?" We get a tremendous amount of fulfillment and joy out of being able to do things like that, and real estate funds that for us.

I start all of my seminars with several "pearls of wisdom," one of which is, "The purpose of life is to truly live before you die. And the purpose of business is to fund that truly perfect life." At the end of the day, that's what you need to remember—real estate is simply the vehicle that funds what you do for and with your family to help you "truly live before you die."

VERY *Important* POINTS

1. The people with whom you align yourself and your business have a dramatic impact on shaping your future. Your relationships with your broker, your clients, other agents, your outside resources, and your family are all very important, and the success of those relationships will ultimately determine your level of success in the real estate business.

2. One of the most vital relationships you will enter into is the company you partner with, or join, as you embark upon your career selling real estate. Use extreme caution and wisdom!

3. When you research real estate companies, search for a solid, professional businessperson who has succeeded in the real estate industry at a very high level. Set the bar high, so that you can succeed at the highest levels too!

4. One of the most valuable pearls of advice we can give you is to mentally picture your life 10 years from now with the broker you are considering.

5. Education is a process, not an event. It is very important to find a company that has ongoing training that offers the next level of education as you grow as an agent.

6. Your clients are the very lifeblood of your real estate business; and your relationships with them should be built on trust, honesty, and commitment to adding value to their lives and to the transaction.

7. A crucial relationship in this industry that has suffered for many years is the connections we build with each other. Other agent relationships are important, and should be treated with respect. We have to be committed to helping each other.

8. Real estate agents who succeed at the highest levels view the industry through an "abundance" mentality instead of a "scarcity" mentality. There is enough business out there for all of us.

VERY Important POINTS

9. The relationship between real estate agents and their affiliates has changed over the years to more of a partnership—one in which they are mutually committed to helping each other grow.

10. A great agent/builder relationship can be extremely successful for both parties.

11. A good title company and a good mortgage company may be the best partners you can have as a real estate professional, either as a new agent or as a more experienced agent, because their goals so closely resemble yours.

12. Your family is the most important relationship you have, and it is the one you need to nurture and protect more than any other. In reality, your family is usually your ultimate reason for building your real estate business.

13. You can't manufacture more hours in each day, so you need to learn very quickly how to be extremely efficient with your time so you can spend more of it with your family.

14. When you are first starting out, it is crucial that you pull your family together and explain to them that you are starting a new business and that you will be working a lot of hours and spending more time away from home—in the beginning. Motivate your family to help you succeed.

15. As you become more successful and build your referral and allied resource database, you'll learn how to better manage and leverage your time.

16. "The purpose of life is to truly live before you die. And the purpose of business is to fund that truly perfect life." At the end of the day, that's what you need to remember—real estate is simply the vehicle that funds what you do for and with your family to help you "truly live before you die."

10

Your Team

*"To succeed at business at the highest level,
it will have to be done with or through others."*
LINDA McKISSACK

**Every one of the seven-person panel of top real
estate producers at the seminar had said we needed
to do it.** We knew we had no choice, but it was such a huge decision for us. When we got back home, we did it. In blind faith, we bit
the bullet and hired our first assistant. We hired a college student,
not knowing how in the world we were going to pay her because we
were still so far in debt. But we just knew that if that many on the
panel of top producers said the same thing, it must work. They were
right. Within months, our business had doubled!

Wow, what a journey it has been since that time! I can still vividly
remember how frightened we were when we hired that first assistant.

I remember all the questions and limiting beliefs: "How will we pay her?" "What will she do?" "What will happen if business goes down?" "I don't have time to train her, so how will she know what to do?" Most people in the real estate business share those same fears. I always tell people not to compare your inside with someone else's outside. If you looked at me now with a team of 13 and thought I could never have been afraid to hire someone, you would be dead wrong. I was terrified! There's just something very frightening about giving up both the control and the money to hire people, especially for the first time. Just the thought of being responsible for a person's salary for the entire year makes most agents very apprehensive about hiring someone. In reality, though, you are only responsible for 90 to 120 days of that person's pay because that is how long it will take you to determine whether he or she is going to change your life.

As a real estate agent, you must focus on four things to make money:

- Working with buyers
- Working with sellers
- Prospecting for buyers and sellers and great people for your team
- Negotiating contracts

All of the other myriad of tasks can be hired out at so much an hour, so you have to ask yourself if it is really dollar productive for you to be doing them. You'll actually find that the sooner you hire someone to do all of those other tasks, the faster your business will grow. When you study successful people, you will find that they are good about building social capital, and succeeding with relationships within the industry. To this day, recruiting and training new team members are not my favorite things to do, but when you are in business for yourself, you will always be doing both.

Just a word of caution: If you are going to share an assistant with someone, make sure you have a set schedule for the hours that person will work for you each day. Before we hired our first full-time assistant, I shared one with two other agents. But even though I was paying a third of her salary, I never really got any benefit from it. I was always out working, and every time I came in to the office, she was busy working for the other two. Our business would have grown much faster during that time if we had determined up front what hours she was to work for each of us.

When you get ready to hire your first employee, your whole paradigm changes from that of a salesperson to that of a business-person. Suddenly, you need to know where you go to find people and what process to go through to make sure they are the right people for the job.

Attracting the Right People

In the beginning, we used the same old methods as everyone else—running an ad in the paper and getting a jillion resumes in response. Now we seldom run an ad because we know that the people we get off an ad typically are not the right fit for our office. If you are just hiring your first assistant, we suggest that you go through people you know to find that perfect person for you.

If you have presented your brand well to the public, you will build a great value proposition and people will want to be part of your team. We have now reached the place where we have enough "magnets" in our own company that people are attracted to working for us. We often have people approach us or one of our associates about coming to work for us. Our team members frequently bring in candidates they think will be a fit, and because we have hired the right kind of people, we give a great deal of credence to those they recommend. Remember past clients, affiliates, or current team members can be great sources.

The Interview Process

When you hire people for your staff, it is almost like entering into an intimate relationship with them. So the longer you can "date" the candidates before you hire them, the more you can tell whether they are compatible with your personality and goals. You want to find a process that enables you to present your company in its true light to the candidates and present the candidates in their true light to you.

When I first started interviewing candidates for our staff, I used nothing but "sell and tell." I talked the whole time! I promise you, I actually hired people to work for us with their never having said four or five words! How can you learn about a person when you are doing all the talking?

Now, thankfully, we use a great program Keller Williams developed called the Ten-Step Process. This process actually helps you present in such a way that the people you are interviewing can discover whether the opportunity you have is right for them, and you can discover if they are right for you. Through a set of questions about the candidates' past, we explore our compatibility. Success leaves clues, so we look for past successes.

I always say, "You were born, and then what happened?" Jim likes to take the person back to his or her last formal education and move forward from that point. We look for their highest highs and their lowest lows. We want to find out what they learned from their problems in the past. One of the main things we look for is whether they have a "victim" mentality. If people say, "This and that happened, but that was because of the boss I had at the time," it's a dead giveaway. But if they take responsibility for the hardships in their lives, they will say something like, "You know, that happened; but let me tell you what I did from that." We listen closely to see if they are looking to blame everyone else in their life for what has happened to them. We also ask them what was the best thing that happened to them in high school. If all they can come up with was dating the football queen or the quarterback, we're in trouble right there.

The Ten-Step Process can be presented in two different phases. The first part is a series of questions to see if the person is qualified for the position. It helps determine if it's a good fit for both parties.

Phase Two is where we look for past successes, check references, ask technical questions about the person's past experience, and find out how they are qualified to do the job for us. When we do a reference check, we go three levels deep. People usually list as references those who know them and like them. We consider that the first level. When we make those calls, we ask the people giving the reference if they know anyone else with whom this person may have worked. We get those second-level names and phone numbers, and we call them. Then we do the same thing and go down one more level. That way, we find out who the candidate really is.

During the second phase of the Ten-Step Process, we also ask the candidate to define his or her vision. We want to know where they see themselves in five or 10 years. *We want people who have high expectations for their own lives because that means they will use our company as a vehicle to help them accomplish their goals.* The more they succeed in their own goals, the more we succeed as a company. We also deal with mutual expectations and compensation, and we do a couple of behavioral assessments as well. One great thing we discover through those assessments is whether they are learning-based. If they are not learning-based, we don't hire them, period. If they don't want to grow as an individual, they won't help us grow as a company.

We have also learned to look at the values of the people we hire during the process because values are very relevant in a relationship. I once had a fellow agent tell me about a person he was having a difficult and actually dysfunctional relationship with. He couldn't understand why—because she was a natural leader for his office. Then one day I was looking for a book for my son in the children's section at the library. He has dyslexia and I wanted to find a book about success-ful people who have had learning disabilities, so I could share their stories with him. The book I found was about Ross Perot. One of the things he said in the book really got my attention: "People's personal values matter." He went on to ask, "If a person is disloyal to the most important commitment he has ever been asked to make in his life, which is his marriage, what makes you think he will ever be loyal to you?" That really hit me. I thought of the situation my colleague had been discussing with me. Perot's comment made me realize that people don't just turn their heads around when they come to work. If we don't have common values outside of work, we won't have common values at the office either. That was a huge lesson for me. I shared it with my colleague as well.

It's good if you can spread the process out over several visits, so you can spend more time with the candidates. Our philosophy is date, date, date. We have even paid them to come in for half a day on Saturday, so we can see them involved in the action. Otherwise, all you will see of them is their best face as it is presented to you on that first day you interview them. The cost of a bad hire is extremely expensive when you look at what it actually costs in lost productiv-ity. So the due diligence you do in the hiring process is time very well spent. And we have learned to hire people on our timetable, not theirs. If someone is pushing us for a hiring decision because they have another offer, we let them go. Typically, every time we have skipped some of the steps and violated our process, we have regretted it later.

We have actually added an eleventh step to our Ten-Step Process, which is the final determining factor. John Maxwell defined it best on one of his audio tapes: *"You can't lead whom you don't love."* I think one of the biggest paradigm shifts for us in hiring people for our team has been that we must hire people we would love to have at our home on the weekends.

I have a team leader who always comes to meetings in one of our other locations. She had a lady working for her, but she was not bringing her with her to the meetings. Recently, I asked why she had not come, and my team leader said, "Linda, I just couldn't stand to have her ride over here with me." That relationship ended just a short time later, as it should have.

One of the things I have learned from working with a team is that you can't lie awake at night worrying about people who are not lying awake at night worrying about you! If that commitment isn't there on their side, it just isn't going to work.

Hiring the "Right" People

Once you hire that first assistant and he is the right person, you will never go backward and do business like you did before. You will always move forward and take that next step. When you do hire your first assistant, though, watch your numbers carefully. If your business doesn't increase within a 12-month period, you might consider that you have hired the wrong person or you may not be using the extra time to generate leads.

When we first started hiring our team, we hired people to support us. Now we hire people to replace us. For some reason, real estate agents often think they don't want to be replaced because they believe that no one can do the job as well as they can. After I had been with another company for five years, it suddenly dawned on me one day that very few people ever called and asked for the owner of the company. That was my first "ah-ha" realization that other people could actually meet with my clients and do things in my place. It didn't all have to be me. If I hired great quality people who met the clients' needs, that's all that really mattered. The biggest limitation that most real estate agents have is their selves. They don't allow themselves to go to the next level. The idea that "no one can do it better than me" is wrong. There are many people who can, and who are even more qualified. That concept was a huge paradigm shift for us, and we began to look for dynamic people who could actually replace us, rather than just support us. And we have also learned to look for people who can manage us, rather than our having to manage them. Some agents want to hire people they can dictate to and control, rather than those who will partner with them so they can grow.

I heard John Maxwell suggest not long ago that business owners put a chart on their wall with the names of all the people in their organization, and then put a letter beside each person representing how impacted their business would be should they leave. There should be at least five to seven big "ouches" on the chart—people they can't afford to lose. These covenant relationships are very, very important to your business.

Another thing Gary did at that same seminar was go around the room, which was full of Keller Williams' top producing agents in the country (nearly everyone in there made at least $1,000,000 in commission a year), and have each agent tell how much their highest paid salaried (not commissioned) person made. Most people in the room said something like $30,000 or $40,000. At the time, we had the highest paid person of anyone in the room, at about $100,000, until we got to Gary Keller. Most of his key people made more than $200,000! But what was so incredibly amazing was that, as we observed the dynamics of each person in the room, it was obvious that their quality of life very closely correlated with how much they paid their key people! The lower the pay scale for their people, the lower their quality of life! Those who were willing to hire people who deserved to be paid an extremely high salary had more time off, more freedom, and a higher amount of passive income (less work for the money). That realization was another epiphany for us, and it moved us more toward finding people who were very, very talented and those who could replace us rather than just support us.

In the National Best-seller *The Millionaire Real Estate Agent*, Gary along with authors Dan Jenks and Jay Papasan, identified seven levels of a real estate business:

Level One: You work alone
(typically less than 15–20 listings)

Level Two: You hire your first assistant
(20–25 listings)

Level Three: You hire your second assistant
(25–40 listings)

Level Four: You hire your first buyer agent
(25–40 listings)

Level Five: You hire one more assistant and a few
more buyer agents
(50 or more listings)

Level Six: You hire a listing specialist who helps
you manage your business
(50 or more listings)

Level Seven: You replace yourself
(you step out of the business and
start opening other businesses)
(50 or more listings)

These listing numbers are a function of the average selling price (ASP). The higher the ASP, the lower the number of listings required to support additional staff. In any case, you should hire additional staff as soon as you can, as soon as your business can support the costs.

There are different rules of thumb as to when you should add these different people to your staff. When you are doing paperwork until 8 or 9 at night, or you are not finding time to get back in touch with your buyers and sellers on a timely basis and your quality of service is going down, it's time to hire an assistant. When your leads are falling in the trash can, it's time to hire a sales person. Your listings are also a good barometer.

Performance Standards

Once you hire people for your team, you must establish standards for their performance. When I first brought my key people on, I was always mad and I wasn't sure why. I called my mentor and talked to him about it, and he asked, "What are the standards you expect of them?" I told him I really didn't know. "You have to have standards," he told me. "Otherwise, they don't know how they are performing, and you don't know how they are performing." I took his advice, and what a difference it made with my team! You establish the standards, like the number of calls to make, the number of buyer or seller contracts to write, etc. Then you present those standards to your team and hold them accountable. You don't have to worry about how they are doing it, as long as they are doing it with high values and integrity.

Jim hired a man to be a team leader in one of our offices in another state. He was a great guy, and Jim really liked him. But he was holding him accountable to the standards of the office: recruiting so many agents a month, maintaining a certain percentage of profitability, and keeping agent retention at a certain level. In order to make those things happen, there were a certain number of tasks he had to do each week or each month (prospecting, etc.) Over a six-month period, he was consistently behind on his numbers. Unfortunately, Jim had to let him go. Because they had a great relationship, the man knew it wasn't a personal thing, and they are still friends today. It was just the fact that he wasn't meeting his standards, and he was probably better suited to go and do something else. Jim really just consulted him out of a job. Now, has it always worked out like that? Unfortunately, we have had relationships in the past where we didn't hold people accountable. When Jim had to let them go, it became very personal on both sides. We didn't have standards that Jim could point to and say, "This has nothing to do with relationship, but everything to do with your not meeting your standards." We've come a long way since then because we have found that it's a lot harder to fire than it is to hire.

In fact, that is a fear that many agents have—that the people they hire won't work out and they will have to fire them. My daughter Bailey said to me one time, "Mom, I just don't think I could ever fire someone." She understands all about behavioral matching, so I asked her, "Bailey, if a person is not doing well on her job, do you think she is behaviorally matched for the job or not behaviorally matched for the job?" She replied, "Probably not behaviorally matched." I said, "So if she is not doing what she is behaviorally matched to do, do you think she is a happy person or not so happy?" "She's probably not very happy," she said. "Exactly," I told her. "You are not doing her a favor by keeping her in a position in which she is not succeeding because she is probably not very happy, anyway." With the Ten-Step Process we use now, we are pretty confident when we hire people that they are matched to the job.

You've Hired the Right Person—Now What?

After you hire someone and set the standards for that person's performance, you have to let go of the job. I remember calling Gary

Keller from time to time to complain about someone on our team, and he would always ask the same question: "Do you want the job, or do you want that person to have the job?" What I was hoping, of course, was that the person would do the job exactly my way, but that's not the question. Agents like myself who want to control the way everything is done have to remember to constantly ask themselves that same question: "Do I want the job, or do I want that person to have it?" Then give the person permission to fail. I used to tell my assistant, "As long as you don't cost me all of my commissions all of the time, we are going to be okay." It was an overstatement, of course, and she knew it. But it was my way of telling her that if she made a mistake and it cost me some money, then we were just going to fix it. *You must empower your people to do their jobs, make decisions, and make mistakes.* That's really what building a team is all about: Presenting with the right process to find the right people, believing that you have found the right people, and then allowing them to do their jobs, whether they make a mistake or not, so you can both grow to new heights of success.

Another concern some agents have is how to train the people they hire. *Once you make the decision to bring someone on to your team, you have to be willing to believe you have hired the right person and then spend the time and effort to train him or her.* We put together a 90-day training plan for every employee we bring on board. You also have to be sure your people are growing through outside learning opportunities. We can't stress enough that you can't grow your organization with people who are not learning based. If they are not interested in growing themselves, they won't help your company grow.

We have discovered that people will generally only do what they self-discover. The best way to get them to self-discover is to take them with you when you go to classes and seminars. (This step is usually a hard one for real estate agents.) Sit them beside you and let them have their own "ah-has." Let them self-discover what they need to do—what their role is in what you are learning to help take the team to the next level. After the seminar, have a brainstorming session with them to see what their action plan is, based on what they learned. We have found that people often see more value in an organization that has invested in their growth through learning opportunities than one that just pays the higher dollars. In the beginning, we didn't take our assistants with us when we attended training events and seminars. We would go to these meetings and get all excited about what we learned, and we would come home and "regurgitate" all over everyone with our excitement and the new ideas we learned. Eventually, our team got to where they dreaded seeing us come back. If you take your people with you and get them involved in the training, they get excited, too!

We also have very clear job descriptions for each role on our team, and each position has a manual. In the beginning, we just assigned them tasks to do, and we gave them the responsibility of writing their own job descriptions. I will say, though, that because we had great systems, the job descriptions almost wrote themselves.

Remember that you don't have to have all the right answers for your people; you just have to have the right questions. I used to really fret over trying to have all the answers for everyone on my team. Then I realized that they actually have the answers. I just have to ask the right questions in the right way until they discover the answers themselves. (Remember, people learn best when they self-discover.)

When you hire someone for your team, you must care about the whole person. Some agents operate in fear that their people will find out what they do and how they do it, and then leave and compete against them. And because of their fear, they don't let their people grow into the next opportunity. There are two things you have to realize: 1) Some are going to come and stay, and some are going to go, and 2) *Most talented people leave when they feel that there is no more opportunity available for them.* If that talented person looks up and sees that the next position he feels he is ready for is yours, and he doesn't think you are ever going to be willing to grow out of your job and give it to him, he will leave you. He will go where there is opportunity. If a talented person looks up and sees that there is a child or a family member poised to take that next position, he will realize that there is no room for him to grow and will leave. It's very important to care about your people as a whole and constantly be looking out for the next opportunity for them to grow into.

Interaction with Your Team

When you bring a new person into your company, the first thing you want to do is sit down with them and present your company's vision, mission, values, and goals. Then, for the first 100 days a new person is on board, we recommend that you almost micromanage them by measuring daily what they do. Because you want to hold them pretty accountable for those first 100 days, you will need to spend time with them every day. After the first 100 days, you can go to a consultative-type meeting with them once a week. By this time you know they have the ability to meet their standards, and you are now just holding them accountable for results. Since we hire people who can manage us instead of those whom we have to manage, they take more ownership of their jobs, and we don't have to spend a whole lot of time with them after the first 100 days.

When you hire your first assistant, you will probably need to spend an hour or so a day with that person for the first 100 days, during which you will focus on systems training and the tasks they need to be doing. After the first 100 days, you will need to schedule a consultative meeting with them for five or 10 minutes at the beginning of each day.

In these weekly and daily meetings with our people, we use a Keller Williams form, called 4-1-1, as an accountability sheet. It has a place to write your goals for the year and then for each month. Then it has a place to list all of the tasks that need to be accomplished each week in the month to help achieve the monthly goal, which achieves the yearly goal. We hold our people accountable to the goals on that sheet.

The higher the talent and the more a person contributes to the income of the business, the more intimate your relationship will be with that person. You will be very involved in the lives of your key people, because you are looking out for their future and trying to help them figure out how to build wealth. We own rental houses in a partnership with some of our key people because we know they need to build passive income and they may not be comfortable doing it on their own.

Important POINTS

1. If you want to grow big, you need people to help you get there.

2. If you have presented your brand well to the public, you will build a great value proposition and people will want to be part of your team.

3. When you hire people for your staff, it is almost like entering into an intimate relationship with them. So the longer you can "date" the candidates before you hire them, the more you can tell whether they are compatible with your personality and goals. You want to find a process that enables you to present your company in its true light to the candidates and to present the candidates in their true light to you.

4. You want to hire people who have high expectations for their own lives because that means they will use your company as a vehicle to help them accomplish their goals. The more they succeed in their own goals, the more you succeed as a company.

5. Look at the values of the people you hire during the process because values are very relevant in a relationship.

6. You can't lead whom you don't love.

7. You may have started out hiring people to support you, but you need to hire people to replace you.

8. Wealthy business people usually have five to seven key people who are responsible for the bulk of the money that comes into their businesses.

9. Those who are willing to hire people who deserve to be paid an extremely high salary usually have more time off, more freedom, and a higher amount of passive income.

10. Once you hire people for your team, you must establish standards for their performance. Then present those standards to your people and hold them accountable. You don't have to worry about how they are doing it, as long as they are doing it with high values and integrity.

Conclusion

A Matter of the Heart

When Linda and I were first associated with Keller Williams Realty, working in a franchise agency, Linda was the number one agent in Denton, Texas, and the Keller Williams office with which we were affiliated had over 40 percent of the market share in the Denton area. For some reason, our owner-broker (with whom we thought we had a close relationship) made the decision not to renew her franchise agreement with Keller Williams. She tried to recruit all of the agents to make the change with her to what she believed was a more established, traditional franchise, where she thought we could all make more money. But Linda and I really enjoyed our association with Keller Williams. We had already begun cultivating and nurturing that relationship, and we liked the culture, the training, and the economic model (how much money we paid to the company). After careful due diligence we made the decision that the move to this traditional company would not be right for us. Because Keller Williams had taught us that *we* were the brand, we had no interest in paying more money to be with a larger real estate company that presented *itself* as the brand.

Our broker-owner's franchise agreement was up in September of 1996. By June of that year, she wanted to know who was staying with her and who was leaving. We advised her that we would not be making the move, and in July we opened our own real estate business, called McKissack Real Estate Services.

In September of 1996, as our former broker-owner relinquished her affiliation with Keller Williams, we made the decision to purchase the franchise in Denton. What appeared to be a challenge that was happening *to* us turned out to be the "blessing" that changed our lives forever! The relationships we have built because of that one decision are unbelievable. What a blessing it is to have Gary Keller as a mentor and coach. He helped move us to the seventh, or top level of the real estate business and completely convert our "sales jobs" into a "sales business" that has gone from $25 million in 1996 to over $60 million in 2006! What wonderful relationships we have developed with our partners in Florida, Texas, Colorado, Ohio, Kentucky, and Indiana! These relationships are deep and abiding because they are based upon presentations from the heart and steeped in trust!

Our best lessons as real estate agents have come from our relationships. Besides evolving from agents in a sales job to businesspeople in the business of real estate, we have learned so much. We've learned to "Think big, be different, and be bold. Get out of your box and out of your own way." If you, too, choose to take the path to turn your sales job into an asset-based business, you will need to load your toolbox. You will have to learn to think like a CEO. You will have to learn business skills.

Another lesson that Linda heard loud and clear from many other relationships early on in her career was the truth that "You must list to last" in this business. We firmly believe that another reason our real estate business has been so successful is our focus has always been on *listings*. We learned to build all of our lead generation systems around getting saleable listings because *great saleable listings bring great qualified buyers*. Remember, the three L's of real estate are: Leads, Listing, and Leverage.

When Linda is out teaching and speaking, she often makes this statement: "If you don't design your own perfect life, someone will design it for you." So we encourage you to be proactive and design your own perfect life. Be responsible for your life and career. Never compromise your values or standards for anyone. Build your relationships from the heart, and then learn from those relationships. You might even consider looking for a coach or a consultant to help hold you accountable for reaching your goals. Tony is our business consultant, and we have learned so much from him. Our relationship with him is invaluable, and we certainly consider it a tremendous blessing!

As you work with a coach or consultant, or even as you attend seminars and read books like this one, the more you apply the principles you learn, the faster your business will grow. The time you spend on developing yourself will be the secret weapon that pushes you over the top. Work on your leadership skills. No one is a born leader; you must develop those skills.

There is another pivotal relationship of the heart that must be built on trust, honesty, and integrity—your relationship with yourself. Your success in life depends on how you feel about yourself—period. But if you are to be successful in real estate, you must also look deeply within and ask *why* you want to build this business. What are the personal drivers that keep you going, day after day? If you haven't yet discovered the main thing that impacts the force with which you are building your real estate business, you may not have mastered the art of presenting well to yourself—from your heart. You are your most important and most challenging audience. Presenting well to convince the one who knows you best is an ingenious feat, and one that must be repeated often.

Until you can identify your personal drivers and desires with confidence and assurance, you will bounce around from pillar to post—experimenting, tasting, testing, exploring. That's fine until you're ready to settle down and become successful. If you're ready—really ready—to get serious about being the best agent you can be, it's time to stop bouncing and think about the following questions: "Why am I building this business? What is it, exactly, that will propel me to get out there day after day and do the hard things—those things that the average real estate agent won't do; the things that are important to building this business?"

Perhaps you want to send your children to college, or to get out of debt, or buy a new home. Or maybe it's deeper than that: to prove to yourself that you really can be successful. If you've already answered that question and you are reading this book for the extra edge that will take your business to the next level—congratulations!

The thing that kept us going in the beginning was that we had gotten in debt, and wanted to get out, and we also wanted to send our daughter to a Christian school and then to a Christian college. But as the years went by, we found another reason that fueled our desire to work hard, and it's proved to be the engine that drives our success: *We love to be able to give to other people.* There is never a negative or bad repercussion from giving to other people. Amazingly, the more we give, the more we get. It's the principle of sowing and reaping. You cannot seem to "out give" what you get. You can't always put a dollar figure on it. Our lives have been enriched, our bank accounts have gone up, and our success in every other area has increased when we have helped other people and not focused on what is in it for us. In the long run our lives have been truly enriched, monetarily and in every other way, by giving to other people. It feeds a piece of us that money can never feed.

This message is something that Linda and I would truly like to convey to other real estate agents. We have found that the real estate industry as a whole can be considered a greedy industry that operates with a scarcity mentality. But Linda and I have learned to do everything from abundance. Enough business exists out there for everyone. As an industry, we have to stop closing our doors and hiding our secrets. We have over 130 agents in one office in Denton, Texas and more than 250 in our office in Flower Mound, Texas. We teach those people to do exactly what we are doing. They are independent contractors, so the buyers and sellers can either hire them or they can hire us. In that sense, we are "competitors." But we teach them exactly what to do and how to do it, and this is what happens: When they do what we have taught them to do, their lives get better, they do more business, and they become very grateful for what we have done for them. So nothing bad ever comes from doing something good for someone. Our real estate business has prospered to the point that we have one of the most successful practices in the industry. We don't say that boastfully, and we don't take our success lightly. We are grateful for the success, but we also gratefully acknowledge the support, knowledge, and advice that others have poured into us. That's what relationships built on presentations from the heart will do.

Linda and I are ordinary people from ordinary backgrounds. If we can build a multi-million dollar real estate business, so can you. Use your God-given talents and build your relationships on presentations from your heart. Success is a lot more about the journey than the destination.

JIM AND LINDA MCKISSACK

About the Authors

LINDA AND JIM MCKISSACK

LINDA AND JIM MCKISSACK are a powerhouse team as two of the nations premier real estate wealth building and strategic coaches. The McKissack Realty Group, has been the #1 selling agency in properties SOLD in Denton county and North Texas for more than a decade. The McKissack Realty Group has consistently ranked in the top 10 for Keller Williams Realty Internationally in sales and production. Through their dynamic consulting and strategy sessions with entrepreneurs and realtors, the McKissacks help others transform their lives and take their business to the next level—beyond just the day-to-day income stream most realtors achieve. The McKissacks thriving Real Estate practice consistently sells over $60 million in volume and closes in excess of 375 units each year. They have created over 8 Passive Streams of income and enjoy helping others be successful. Linda and Jim offer Success Coaching, Conference Speaking, and Unique Strategic Facilitation Sessions. To learn more about the principles that can change your life and help you achieve your dreams and for more information on the McKissack's products and services, please contact the authors today at www.PresentationMasteryforRealtors.com

About the Authors

TONY JEARY

Tony Jeary is known across the globe as Mr. Presentation™—the leading authority on Presentation Mastery™. He is the personal coach of CEOs and presidents at Ford Motor Company, EDS, Texaco, Shell, Wal-Mart, SAM's Club, Qualcomm, and New York Life. He has mentored business leaders in thirty-six countries on five continents.

His organization, Tony Jeary High Performance Resources, designs and develops unique products and services to enable their clients to accelerate their success . . . personally and professionally. Tony's focus includes fostering Presentation Mastery™, a business movement that pivots on the concept of strategically elevating the art of presentations. He advises his clients to establish the role of Chief Presentation Officer (CPO) in order to harness the power of presentations at all levels.

In order to be near his family, he often works from his studio, a half-million-dollar presentation laboratory. The studio provides his high achieving clients with a unique, private setting in which to create some of the world's most influential presentations. Here he deploys more than two decades of dedicated research and best practices to forward the strategic agendas of both individuals and organizations.

Tony is dedicated to his motto, "Give value, do more than expected." He believes that life really is a series of presentations, and his new vision is to inspire all people to use Presentation Mastery™ to enhance their effectiveness and quality of life.

Tony is a devoted husband and the father of two daughters. He lives just outside of Dallas, Texas. He is committed to furthering the success of his church and community.

For more information on his products and services you can visit his website at www.TonyJeary.com or email info@TonyJeary.com.

Other Tony Jeary Resource Materials

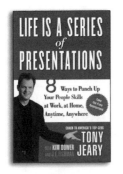

Life Is a Series of Presentations

Tony's best selling series comes from this title published by Simon and Schuster. Eight best practices to inspire, inform and influence anyone, anytime, anywhere.

The content of this book will dramatically improve your ability to effectively communicate your ideas to individuals or to groups.

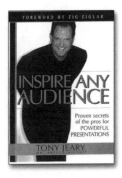

Inspire Any Audience

- Prepare your presentation in half the time
- Solve those nervous jitters
- Exceed audience expectations
- Use tools effectively including flip charts, overheads, handouts, microphones, and more

This title is what Zig Ziglar calls "the ultimate presenter's handbook".

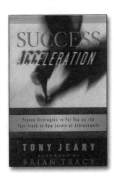

Success Acceleration

Being clear on what you really want, what success is to you and how to accelerate both your personal and professional success is the basis for this foundation title.

- Develop and maintain a winning attitude
- Benchmark winners to accelerate your results
- Plan, set goals and maximize success with maximum speed

For these resources and to take the
FREE Presentation Mastery™ assessment go to:
www.TonyJeary.com